J306.0945 PA
Parks, Peggy
Growing up i

Guelph Public Library
Removed from Inventory
Guelph Public Library MAR 2018

Growing Up AROUND THE WORLD

Growing Up in Italy

Other titles in the *Growing Up Around the World* series include:

Growing Up in Brazil
Growing Up in Canada
Growing Up in China
Growing Up in Germany
Growing Up in India
Growing Up in Iran
Growing Up in Japan
Growing Up in Mexico
Growing Up in Russia

Growing Up AROUND THE WORLD

Growing Up in Italy

Peggy J. Parks

ReferencePoint Press®

San Diego, CA

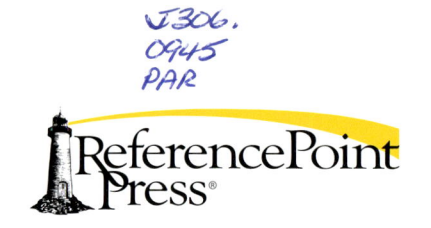

© 2018 ReferencePoint Press, Inc.
Printed in the United States

For more information, contact:
ReferencePoint Press, Inc.
PO Box 27779
San Diego, CA 92198
www.ReferencePointPress.com

ALL RIGHTS RESERVED.
No part of this work covered by the copyright hereon may be reproduced or used in any form or by any means—graphic, electronic, or mechanical, including photocopying, recording, taping, web distribution, or information storage retrieval systems—without the written permission of the publisher.

LIBRARY OF CONGRESS CATALOGING-IN-PUBLICATION DATA

Names: Parks, Peggy J., 1951– author.
Title: Growing Up in Italy/by Peggy J. Parks.
Description: San Diego, CA: ReferencePoint Press, Inc., 2018. | Series: Growing Up Around the World | Audience: Grades 9 to 12. | Includes bibliographical references and index.
Identifiers: LCCN 2017004148 (print) | LCCN 2017016039 (ebook) | ISBN 9781682822180 (eBook) | ISBN 9781682822173 (hardback)
Subjects: LCSH: Italy—Social life and customs—Juvenile literature. | Children—Italy—Juvenile literature. | Youth—Italy—Juvenile literature.
Classification: LCC DG451 (ebook) | LCC DG451 .P35 2018 (print) | DDC 945--dc23
LC record available at https://lccn.loc.gov/2017004148

CONTENTS

Italy at a Glance	6
Chapter One	8
A Country of Beauty and Fascination	
Chapter Two	20
Home and Family	
Chapter Three	31
Education and Work	
Chapter Four	42
Social Life	
Chapter Five	53
Religious Influence	
Source Notes	65
For Further Research	71
Index	73
Picture Credits	79
About the Author	80

ITALY AT A GLANCE

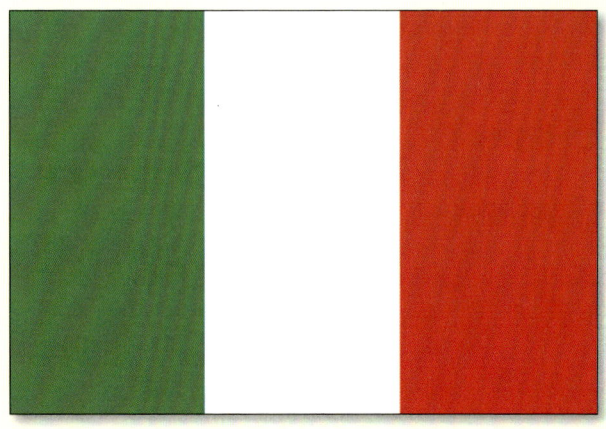

Official Name
Repubblica Italiana (The Italian Republic)

Capital
Rome

Size
Italian Peninsula and islands: 116,275 square miles (301,151 sq. km)

Total Population
59.8 million

Youth Population
0–14 years: 8.4 million

Religion
Primarily Roman Catholic

Type of Government
Parliamentary republic

Language
Italian

Currency
Euro

Industries
Mechanical machinery, textiles, furniture, motor vehicles

Literacy
99% (age 15+ able to read and write)

Internet Users
65.6% of population

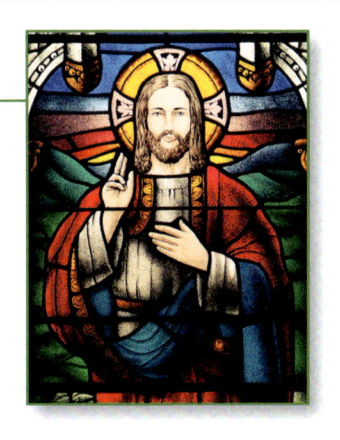

CHAPTER ONE

A Country of Beauty and Fascination

As a professional photographer, Giulio Pugliese has traveled all over the world. He has seen some of the most beautiful places on Earth, but he has no desire to live anywhere but Italy. Pugliese was born and raised in Rome, Italy's capital, a city that he always finds a source of inspiration for his photographs. But as dear as Rome is to Pugliese, he loves all of Italy. He is in awe of the country's breathtaking landscapes, towering mountain ranges, plentiful vineyards, and charming villages. Pugliese says that nothing can compare to how he feels while walking through Italy's countryside or visiting its cities. "The beauty of Italy," he says, "is in its history and in its tradition. . . . Italy is a country that steals your heart."[1] Many Italians, as well as people who have visited Italy, share Pugliese's passion for it, which is why it is one of the world's most beloved countries.

A Diverse Landscape

Located in southern Europe, Italy is affectionately known to Italians as Il Bel Paese, meaning "the Beautiful Country." Another nickname for Italy is Lo Stivale, which means "the Boot," because its main body of land, the Italian Peninsula, is shaped like a long, slender, high-heeled boot. Along with the peninsula, the large islands of Sicily and Sardinia, as well as about seventy smaller islands, are part of Italy. Altogether, the country covers 116,275 square miles (301,151 sq. km), which is an area slightly larger than the US state of Arizona. The peninsula is surrounded by four seas: the Adriatic, Ionian, Ligurian, and Tyrrhenian. Although the sea has its own name, they are all part of the larger Mediterranean Sea.

Italy has numerous prominent physical features, including more than 4,700 miles (7,564 km) of coastline. It is also a country with a rugged landscape of rolling hills and towering mountain ranges. In fact, only about 20 percent of Italy is flat, with the remainder hilly or mountainous. The country has two major mountain ranges: the Apennines, which run through the Italian Peninsula, and the Alps in northern Italy. Monte Bianco, which is Italian for "White Mountain," is part of the Alps and is located on the border between France and Italy. Rising to a height of more

Located in southern Europe, the country of Italy is known to Italians as Il Bel Paese, which means "the Beautiful Country." Its capital, Rome, features many public spaces, including Navona Square (pictured).

than 15,700 feet (4,809 m) above sea level, Monte Bianco is one of the tallest mountain peaks in Europe.

The Apennines are among Italy's most distinctive features. Because they span nearly the entire peninsula, these mountains are often called the spine of Italy. They formed through a geological process known as plate tectonics. According to this theory, Earth's upper crust is made up of gigantic slabs of rock called plates, which float on a churning layer of partially molten rock. The plates are constantly on the move, grinding against each other and sometimes colliding. Such collisions can cause Earth's crust to push upward, which over millions of years forms mountains. In addition, ongoing plate motion can lead to massive cracks in rocks known as faults. These are the points where earthquakes are most likely to occur.

Earthquakes and Volcanoes

Due to its location atop major faults, Italy has a high risk for earthquakes; in fact, it is one of the most earthquake-prone countries in Europe. Over a three-month period in 2016, at least 250 earthquakes struck Italy. In August of that year, a powerful earthquake struck the country's central region. It flattened entire towns, including the historic village of Amatrice, and killed nearly three hundred people. One of the survivors was a little girl named Giorgia Rinaldo, who lay buried in the rubble of a collapsed building for nearly seventeen hours.

In addition to earthquakes, the plate movement beneath Italy contributes to volcanic eruptions. Near the point where the Eurasian and African plates meet sit three major active volcanoes: Etna, Stromboli, and Vesuvius. Etna is located on the east coast of the island of Sicily. At 10,900 feet (3,322 m) above sea level, Etna is the highest active volcano in Europe and has the longest documented eruption history of any volcano in the world. "Because it is erupting almost continuously," says travel writer Ocean Malandra, "the height changes frequently when it blows its top off."[2]

The Stromboli volcano is located on an island of the same name. Known as Mount Stromboli, it bears the distinction of being one of the most active volcanoes in the world. Since 1932 it has erupted almost continuously. Its eruptions range from small

Mount Etna, on the island of Sicily, is one of Italy's major active volcanoes. Etna is the tallest active volcano in Europe and has the longest documented eruption history of any volcano in the world.

explosions about every half hour to large eruptions that occur infrequently. Stromboli's eruptions are often visible over long distances at night, which has led to the volcano being nicknamed the Lighthouse of the Mediterranean.

Of the three active volcanoes, Vesuvius, which overlooks the Bay of Naples on Italy's west coast, is the most famous. It is best known for a catastrophic eruption in 79 CE. The eruption buried the cities of Pompeii and Herculaneum under a deep layer of ash and killed thousands of people. Even today, Vesuvius is considered one of the world's most dangerous volcanoes.

Regional Differences

Although Italy has twenty regions, it is typically divided into three major areas: northern Italy, central Italy, and southern Italy. The regions are very distinctive, with dramatic changes in the landscape and way of life from one region to the next. According to the website Understanding Italy, one of the main factors that makes each Italian region unique is the attitude of the people who live there: "Italians are fiercely loyal to their own region, each believing that theirs is better than any other. . . . They love the landscape of their own home and think their region's climate is the best and steadfastly hang on to every tradition and fragment of culture that is historically theirs."[3] This regional loyalty is so strong and so important to Italians that there is a word for it: *campanilismo*. This refers to a sense of identity, pride, and devotion to one's region, city, town, or village.

Northern Italy is the site of the Lake District, where the crystal blue Lakes Maggiore and Orta are located. It is also the site of the Italian Riviera on the Ligurian Sea, and the pastel-colored cliffside villages of Portovenere, Monterosso, and Vernazza. Martina Vaccari is a young woman who lives in the northern town of Castelgomberto. The town is small and quaint and surrounded by hills. "It's really little and cute," says Vaccari. "I love the architecture. The buildings are very old and they are beautiful."[4] Also in northern Italy is the remarkable city of Venice, located on the coast along the Adriatic Sea. Built on more than one hundred small islands in an Adriatic lagoon, Venice has canals instead of roads, with the Grand Canal serving as the city's main thoroughfare. People travel throughout Venice's canals in water taxis, water buses, or private gondolas.

One of central Italy's regions is Tuscany, where during the summer months the countryside is ablaze with brilliant yellow sunflower fields. Italy's capital city, the ancient, historic Rome, is located in Tuscany, as is Florence. Also in Tuscany is the hillside town of Cortona, which was made famous by author Frances Mayes in her book *Under the Tuscan Sun*. When Mayes first bought her home, Bramasole, in Cortona, the town was quiet and virtually unknown. Today, says Mayes, it is lively and thriving.

The south of Italy, which includes the southern part of the Italian Peninsula and the islands of Sicily and Sardinia, is known as the Mezzogiorno. This traditional name, which means "Midday," refers to the strength of the midday sun in this region. The south's

> "Italians are fiercely loyal to their own region, each believing that theirs is better than any other."[3]
>
> —Understanding Italy, a website about Italy, Italian people, and Italian life

Italy's Archipelagos

Most people are aware of Italy's two main islands, Sicily and Sardinia. Yet numerous smaller islands are also part of Italy, including more than a dozen archipelagos. Pronounced ark-i-PEL-ago, the word refers to a group, chain, or cluster of islands. In the Tyrrhenian Sea, for example, off the coast of Sicily, is the Aeolian archipelago. These islands sit between the volcanoes Vesuvius and Etna and are formed entirely from volcanic rock. The seven islands that make up the Aeolian archipelago include Lipari (the largest), Panarea, Vulcano, Stromboli, Salina, Alicudi, and Filicudi.

There are also seven islands in the Tuscan archipelago, which is off the coast of Tuscany between the Ligurian and Tyrrhenian Seas. These islands are widely known for their breathtaking natural beauty, as Italian writer Gina Mussio explains:

> The islands off Tuscany have some of the most natural, well-preserved flora and fauna in the entire country, with water so crystal you can view schools of fish clear to the bottom. They're so beautiful in fact, that it is said they are gifts from the gods. Legend has it that when the beautiful Venus emerged from the sea, her necklace broke and seven pearls fell, forming the seven Tuscan islands.

Elba is the largest island in the Tuscan archipelago and the third-largest island in Italy after Sicily and Sardinia. The other six islands are Giglio, Capraia, Montecristo, Pianosa, Giannutri, and the tiny island of Gorgona, which covers less than 1 square mile (2.2 sq. km).

Gina Mussio, "Off the Coast of Tuscany: A Guide to the Tuscan Archipelago," *Walks of Italy Blog*, July 4, 2014. www.walksofitaly.com.

---

largest city is Naples, which is on the shores of the Mediterranean Sea. Compared with the rest of Italy, the southern region is more rural, and the lifestyle is more relaxed. "Northern Italy is busier, and the people like to be on time," says Anna Del Magno, a teenage girl from northeastern Italy, who adds that "southern Italy is more leisurely."[5]

Southern Italy also differs from the north in terms of income and quality of life. The northern region tends to be the richest, whereas parts of southern Italy fall far below the European

A woman transports firewood through a narrow street in the southern village of Rodio. Southern Italy has a much higher prevalence of poverty than northern Italy.

average. According to research by the World Bank, income inequality is 15 percent higher in southern Italy than it is in northern Italy. Thus, the south has a much higher prevalence of poverty than the north. "Differences between rich and poor are noticeable," says Marco Scognamiglio, a young man from Bologna. "There is also a vast difference in wealth between the North (richer) and the South (poorer)."[6]

The Many Variations of Language

One of the most prominent differences among Italy's regions is the language people use. Although the country's official language is Italian, people speak a variety of dialects—localized forms of the language that vary widely from region to region. Some of these dialects are so different from standard Italian that they are like another language altogether. "In their daily lives, many Italians don't speak Italian," says journalist Gaia Pianigiani. "That is, they don't shop or chat or argue in standard Italian, the kind that is studied in school and heard on the news. They use one of the country's hundreds of local dialects, each with its own quirks of pronunciation, inflection and vocabulary."[7]

Even though it is not a spoken language, body language is a fundamental part of Italian conversation. "The most important element of communication are the gestures," says Italian writer Nicoletta Di Bartolomeo. "The way we move our hands, hold our heads, move our shoulders, our facial expressions, as well as the way we use our eyes and mouths to make ourselves understood. We simply cannot talk without our hands." Anywhere Italians have conversations, it is common to see them gesturing wildly as they speak—and talking very loudly. "Italians speak very loudly in public whether on the bus, in the street or on the phone," says Di Bartolomeo. "Don't worry, we are not all deaf."[8]

> "Italians speak very loudly in public whether on the bus, in the street or on the phone."[8]
>
> —Italian writer Nicoletta Di Bartolomeo

A girl named Giulia Rotunno says that the gestures Italians use may be offensive to some people. Rotunno was an exchange student in the United States for almost a year. Before leaving Italy, she was told to be careful about using gestures. "Italians are known to use hand gestures a lot," she says, "and in some cultures some of the gestures can be considered rude."[9]

Italy's People

Along with language, physical appearance can also vary widely among Italians based on their native region. Those from Venice in the north, for instance, tend to be taller and thinner than inhabitants of Naples in the south. Many people from the far north have blond hair and blue eyes. This is in stark contrast to the dark brown hair and eyes of those from the Mezzogiorno.

Regardless of the particular region they visit and the people they encounter in it, visitors to Italy are often struck by how friendly, warm, and welcoming Italians are. They often go out of their way to make outsiders feel at home. And while Italians are passionate people who tend to be impatient, they are also charming, and their enthusiasm is contagious. As the travel agency Passion for Italy writes, "Italians on the whole believe in living life to the fullest. They laugh, shout, cry and argue at the top of their voices in public. They are always blasting their horns if you drive too slow. However they never take themselves too seriously and the Italian sense of humour is ever present."[10]

> "Italians on the whole believe in living life to the fullest. They laugh, shout, cry and argue at the top of their voices in public."[10]
>
> —The travel agency Passion for Italy

Artistic Treasures

Italians are justifiably proud of their country's priceless art and architecture, which draws tourists from all over the world every year. This pride is shared among adults and youth alike. Angela Bogotto, a teen from a small northeastern city called Schio, offers her perspective: "I love my country because every little town brings with it centuries of history that are still living through the museums, the ancient buildings and streets."[11]

Italy is home to some of the most famous architectural structures in the world. One example is a freestanding bell tower located in the city of Pisa, in the Tuscany region. Construction on the medieval tower began in 1173, and it took more than two hundred years to complete. During construction, when the foundation stones were laid on ground that was too soft, the tower began to lean. Engineers were unable to correct the problem. In fact, the tower sank further in the soft ground and leaned even more. Over time the ground beneath it compressed, which saved the tower from toppling over. Today it leans at about a 10-degree angle and is known internationally as the Leaning Tower of Pisa.

Another renowned structure is the Colosseum in Rome, which is the largest amphitheater ever built. Constructed in 70 CE of concrete and sand, the Roman Colosseum has eighty arched entrances and once held up to fifty-five thousand spectators, who were seated in order of rank. They watched gruesome entertainment, such as violent gladiator fights, wild animal slaughter, and public executions. "Even today, in a world of skyscrapers, the Colosseum is hugely impressive," said the late British historian Keith Hopkins. "It stands as a glorious but troubling monument to Roman imperial power and cruelty."[12]

One of the most well-known Italian works of art is also the most treasured: the Sistine Chapel in the Apostolic Palace, which is home to the pope. Every surface of the chapel is adorned with artwork. The floors are covered in mosaics, and on the walls are religious scenes done in fresco, a technique in which painting is done on wet plaster. The wall behind the altar was painted by the famous Renaissance artist Michelangelo. He also painted the ceiling of the chapel, and it is one of his most famous and beloved works. From 1508 to 1512, Michelangelo covered the ceiling in frescoed religious scenes. Today, visitors to the Sistine Chapel are often brought to tears as they gaze at the breathtaking artwork that surrounds them.

Government Turmoil

With such amazing works of art, gorgeous scenery, and warm, hospitable people, it is no wonder that Italy is such a beloved country. But it is also a nation that has struggled for years with a tumultuous political climate. Since the 1940s Italy has had several dozen governments. Today, its government is relatively young, with 13 percent of parliament officials under the age of forty (up from 7 percent in 2013). Until December 2016, forty-one-year-old Matteo Renzi held the position of prime minister and was the youngest person of all time to hold that office. Once again, though, the political climate was thrown into turmoil when Renzi resigned after just two and a half years in office.

Renzi was humiliated when voters rejected a series of radical reforms he had proposed to the Italian constitution. After he resigned in response, Parliament approved a new government. Still, uncertainty about the country's political future remains. Sylvia Poggioli, a National Public Radio senior European correspondent based in Rome, says that the Italian political system is one in which "nobody trusts anybody else."[13]

An Aging Population

No matter who holds legislative power, a major concern shared by Italian officials is the country's sluggish population growth. As of 2017, Italy's population was slightly less than 60 million. According to the research organization Euromonitor International, by 2030 the population is expected to grow only modestly, to 62.3 million. During this period, the population will age rapidly, meaning the average age will steadily rise. Based on the average age of its citizens, the report predicts, Italy will be the fourth-oldest country in the world, with more than one-fourth of its citizens over the age of sixty-five. This situation will present many challenges, such as an increased need for government spending on health care and

Passionate Protest

Italy is world renowned for its delicious food, and Italians are proud of their cuisine. They are so proud, in fact, that they have resisted numerous attempts to introduce American food customs in their country. This is what happened in March 1986, when the country's first McDonald's restaurant opened in the Piazza di Spagna, a picturesque city square located in the heart of Rome. Several weeks later, a group called Save Rome staged a protest at the square. Several thousand people gathered for the rally, eager to denounce what they perceived to be the degradation of Italy's food culture. To tout the superiority of traditional Italian fare over McDonald's fast food, attendees were served heaping plates of spaghetti that had been cooked in vast iron skillets. "What disturbs us the most is the Americanization of our life," said Luciano de Crescenzo, an author who attended the rally. "Anyway, Neapolitans have always had their fast food. It's called pizza."

Yet as passionate as they were about ridding Rome of its first fast food restaurant, the protesters' efforts were unsuccessful. The first McDonald's remained in the Piazza di Spagna, and a number of others were opened in the following years.

Quoted in Jennings Parrott, "Big Mac Pasta Protest Boils Over," *Los Angeles Times*, April 21, 1986. http://articles.latimes.com.

social benefit programs for older people. This can strain budgets and hurt economic growth.

One contributing factor to Italy's aging population is the declining birthrate. In 2014 fewer babies were born in the country than in any other year since 1861. "We are very close to the threshold of non-renewal," says health minister Beatrice Lorenzin, "where the people dying are not replaced by newborns. That means we are a dying country." She adds, "We need a wake-up call and a real change of culture to turn the trend around in the coming years."[14]

Another contributor to the aging population is the shrinking population of young adults. Disheartened by the severe job shortage, a growing number of young people are leaving the country. Italy has one of Europe's highest youth unemployment rates—nearly 40 percent in 2016. So when young Italians finish their education and are ready to begin their careers, many feel they have no choice but to look for work in other countries.

Looking Ahead

In the coming years, Italy will need to address a number of issues, from governmental turmoil to its aging population and declining birth rate. But the country has faced crises and challenges throughout its history and has continued to survive and thrive. It is a beautiful, fascinating country resplendent with natural beauty, world-renowned art and architecture, and people who are warm and welcoming. For these and numerous other reasons, Italy holds a special place in the hearts of both native Italians and visitors who fall in love with the country and wish they could stay forever.

CHAPTER TWO

Home and Family

A common saying among people throughout Italy is *La famiglia è tutto*, which means, "The family is everything." The phrase offers insight into how deeply devoted Italians are to their families, and how much their relatives mean to them. "Family is the most important thing in our lives,"[15] says writer Nicoletta Di Bartolomeo. Italians of all ages and all walks of life share that viewpoint. It is instilled in children from a very young age, so they grow up with an understanding of the tremendous value of family love and loyalty.

One indication of this is the close relationships teens have with their parents. It is common for teens and parents to spend time together and to enjoy each other's company. They may share a meal in a café, go out for a dish of rich Italian ice cream known as gelato, or visit with friends in piazzas, which are open public squares in the center of town. Italian families also spend time at home watching television, playing games, or just talking and laughing together. This is how it is for teen Angela Bogotto, who likes to spend time with her family. "I have a very good relationship with my parents, Sergio and Silvana," she says, "and also with my two sisters, Silvia and Marta. We often enjoy talking together."[16]

Family Dynamics

Like families everywhere, Italian families have changed over the years. Yet they are still quite traditional. Although the Italian divorce rate has grown significantly over the years, it is still about half the rate of many other developed countries. According to an international study published in 2015, 89 percent of children in Italy live in households with both parents. This is known as a nuclear family, meaning mother, father, and biological or adopted children living in the same residence.

This sort of traditional family describes the life of a young college student named Jessica from Borgosesia, Italy. She has a close, loving relationship with her parents, Katia and Paolo. "They are both friendly and funny,"[17] says Jessica. Her older sister, Stefania, lives with her boyfriend, but she remains close to the family and visits often with her two dogs.

Traditionally, the Italian father serves as the head of the family, the primary decision maker, and the main breadwinner. Fathers typically have little responsibility for housework or caring for children, although they may pitch in to help. Many Italian men enjoy cooking, but the task of preparing and serving meals falls on the mother. In fact, mothers are responsible for almost every aspect of running the household, including the day-to-day care of the home and family. "On paper, Italian women have equal rights," says Tiziana Bartolini, a magazine editor from Italy. "But reality tells us a different story. Women are expected to care for children."[18] This expectation holds true even as more women are working outside the home. Families who are fortunate enough to be well off financially often employ a housekeeper to handle the bulk of child care and household chores.

Italian children are loved and nurtured. Yet they are also expected to be respectful and responsible. From an early age children are taught to obey rules and mind their parents. "There is an old-fashioned, beautiful sense of love combined with discipline,"[19] says parenting and family expert Liz Fraser. She says the stereotypical image of the Italian family as loud, boisterous, fun, and loving is true, but it is only part of the story. Young Italians are also taught the importance of respect for elders, good manners, and adhering to parents' rules.

> "On paper, Italian women have equal rights. But reality tells us a different story. Women are expected to care for children."[18]
>
> —Tiziana Bartolini, a magazine editor from Italy

Most children and teens help with household tasks, but how much they are required to do varies from family to family. In general, girls help around the house more than boys. One 2016 study found that the extent to which boys assist with household tasks often

Italians are deeply devoted to their families and spend a great deal of time with family members. They may share a meal together or go out for gelato, a frozen dessert that is a favorite Italian treat.

depends on how involved their fathers are with such tasks. Daughters are more likely to assist with domestic chores such as laundry, cleaning up after meals, washing dishes, and tidying the home.

In Anna Del Magno's family, her father does most of the cooking and, in fact, taught her how to cook. The Del Magnos live in Udine, a northern town that lies between the Adriatic Sea and the Alps. Anna's father, who is originally from Rome, taught her how to make lasagna, chicken, and several different types of sauce for pasta. He informed her that she should learn to cook during the summer of 2015, just before she was to travel to the United States as an exchange student. "I have to teach you to cook," her father said, "because you are Italian, and when you get there, they will ask you to cook."[20] And sure enough, says Anna, they did ask, and she enjoyed cooking her father's specialties for them.

The Extended Family

When Italians talk about family, they are often referring to a larger group of relatives beyond the nuclear family. People typically share a close relationship with extended family members, including grandparents, aunts, uncles, and cousins (first, second, and more). They see each other at family gatherings and get together as often as they possibly can.

Many children have close, loving relationships with their grandparents. In some parts of Italy it is common for grandparents to be closely involved with raising children and to play a role in their upbringing. An English teacher who worked with two different families in Italy observed this, and it made a positive impression on her. "The children's grandparents would visit often, especially in the evenings and would stay for dinner, would help to look after the children whilst the parents cooked," she says. "I really liked this element of family life, the families were so close and it was nice to see such a huge influence from an older generation on the lives of the younger ones."[21]

The Strong Family Bond

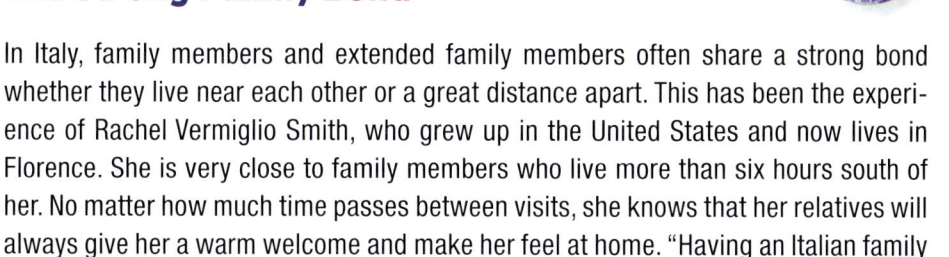

In Italy, family members and extended family members often share a strong bond whether they live near each other or a great distance apart. This has been the experience of Rachel Vermiglio Smith, who grew up in the United States and now lives in Florence. She is very close to family members who live more than six hours south of her. No matter how much time passes between visits, she knows that her relatives will always give her a warm welcome and make her feel at home. "Having an Italian family means you are part of a bond that time, distance and differences [do] not separate," says Smith.

During one visit, Smith went to the cemetery with her family, where they reverently "introduced" her to relatives she had never met. "I was invited to say prayers, kiss my hands and place the kiss upon their [tomb] as if I had known them every day of my life," she says, "because family is family. The bond is that strong."

Rachel Vermiglio Smith, "5 Characteristics of an Italian Family," Iceberg Project, May 13, 2015. http://icebergproject.co.

Michela Gatto, a young woman who was born and raised in Italy, has fond memories of living close to her grandparents as she was growing up. They owned a farm, and she spent much of her childhood playing there. "We had no ipads," says Gatto, "but there were lots of chickens to run after."[22]

Sharing a Home

Although the practice is less common today than in the past, extended family members sometimes live together in the same home. Journalist Patrick Browne, who writes for an Italian newspaper, says it is not out of the ordinary for more than one generation to live under one roof. The sharing of a home by parents, children, grandparents, and sometimes other family members, says Browne, is "a tradition founded on strong family values and the virtue of taking care of each other."[23] Families throughout Italy may share a home with extended family members, but it occurs much more often in the southern regions.

When families make the decision to live together in the same home, one of the biggest incentives is saving money. In general, Italians do not favor the practice of running up large amounts of debt. Although home mortgages are not uncommon, most people are careful not to buy a bigger and more elaborate home than they can afford. Thus, sharing a home benefits them because it allows them to reduce housing costs.

Keeping costs down is a major reason the Morelli family shares a large home in the northern city of Turin. Giuseppe Morelli, a teacher in his forties, lives there along with his parents, his thirty-six-year-old brother, and his nephew, who is in his twenties. "For us, it makes complete sense," says Morelli. "We live together, but independently." He adds that sharing a home has many advantages for the family: "It works well as it means we can keep an eye on our parents and look out for each other."[24]

Slow to Leave the Nest

It is also common for young adults to live with their parents much longer than is typical of other cultures. Many young Italians do not leave home until they are at least in their twenties or thirties or until they get married. A 2014 report by the research organization Eurofound showed that 79 percent of young Italians aged eigh-

The responsibility of childcare falls primarily to women in Italian families. Here, a mother shops for fruit with her young daughter.

teen to thirty live with their parents. In many cases this is the living situation that suits everyone in the family. "Parents really love to have their children (even if the child is 30-years-old) at home,"[25] says Luisa Angaroni, a young Italian woman.

With Italy's failing economy, many young adults live with their parents because they cannot yet afford to live independently. This is the case with Gaia Paradiso, a woman in her twenties from the northern Italian city of Piacenza. She is living in her parents' home while she searches for a job. Paradiso says there are advantages and disadvantages to this arrangement. One of the biggest benefits is the love and support she receives from her parents. Also, being able to live at home helps ease the stress of

An Incentive to Have Babies

Italians are well known for being devoted to their families. People often believe in the stereotype of the Italian family consisting of a father, a mother, and a large brood of children. But even though that was once the norm, it is rarely the case anymore. The country's birth rate has steadily declined over the years, and today it is half of what it was during the 1960s. In fact, Italy now has the lowest birth rate of all the European countries. This is alarming to government officials and the health ministry—so alarming that they offer a cash bonus for having babies. "If we carry on as we are and fail to reverse the [low birth rate] trend," says health minister Beatrice Lorenzin, "there will be fewer than 350,000 births a year in 10 years' time, 40 percent less than in 2010—an apocalypse."

Critics of the baby bonus program claim it will do little to stimulate Italy's low birth rate because too many other factors dissuade people from having multiple children. One is the country's extraordinarily high unemployment rate; most young people will not even consider starting a family if they cannot find a job. Another is the lack of support for women in the workforce, including a shortage of quality child care and employers that do not offer flexible hours for working mothers.

Quoted in Angela Giuffrida, "Why Italy's Facing a Birth Rate Apocalypse," *Local*, May 17, 2016. www.thelocal.it.

job hunting. "So when you wake up, you have your cappuccino; then you start working and you apply for jobs," says Paradiso. "You don't have to worry about the management of the house, which is nice."[26]

Where Italians Live

The homes or apartments where people live vary based on what they can afford and the region of the country where they live. Region is an important factor because of variations in climate. In northern Italy, for instance, it is much colder than in the central or southern parts of the country. So homes in the north are insulated to retain heat. In the far northern regions, where heavy snow is typical during the winter, many homes have deeply sloped roofs to prevent snow from building up. In contrast, most homes in the south are white with terraced roofs. This is also a feature necessitated by climate because temperatures in this region can be very hot. White exteriors reflect sunlight and heat, and this keeps the inside of houses cooler. Flat roofs are also useful for collecting rainwater, which can be essential in areas that are plagued by drought. Houses in Italy are typically made from concrete or brick and sometimes stone.

In most cities Italians live in apartments. Often these are buildings that are five to seven stories high and are divided into individual units known as flats. Few people who live in cities own their own homes with fenced-in yards, says Tommaso Giacomino, a teen from Rome. "We have tall buildings with two, three apartments each floor and no courtyards or garages," he says. "Because of these we have more concentrated towns where there's no need to drive the car every day."[27]

Family, Food, Fellowship, and Fun

Almost any Italian would agree that when a family gets together, food is going to be involved—probably a lot of food. Italians are known for being devoted to their families and for loving food, so combining the two is perfectly natural and normal. "A large part of an Italian family's social life involves eating and celebrating together," says retired educator and writer Alison Jean Thomas. "They meet in bars, pizzerias and restaurants, and frequently share meals in the home."[28]

These get-togethers often seem celebratory, even if the family is not celebrating a holiday or other special occasion. Sitting down at the dinner table with family, says the Italian cooking group Tuscookany, can be "a beautiful celebration of life itself."[29]

> "A large part of an Italian family's social life involves eating and celebrating together."[28]
>
> —Alison Jean Thomas, a writer and retired educator

Italians are in no hurry to finish eating. On the contrary, a family meal is considered an event to be savored, appreciated, and lingered over. It is typical to stay at the table for two hours or longer.

Many families gather for a meal together on Sundays—a meal that they call lunch but could more aptly be called a feast. Even as times have changed and some old Italian customs have fallen by the wayside, the Sunday lunch, or *pranzo della domenica*, remains a lasting tradition. "To Italians, food is everything," says the restaurant Al Bacio. "And on Sunday in particular, food is the centrepiece of the day. As the week slows down, friends and families gather together for a leisurely Sunday lunch to enjoy delicious food and great company."[30]

Although the specific foods served during the meal often vary, the traditional Sunday lunch includes several courses that are brought to the table one by one. The first course is antipasti (appetizers), which is typically cheeses, salami, bruschetta (bread with olive oil, garlic, and tomatoes), and possibly seafood. The second course is usually a homemade pasta dish, followed by a third course of chicken, rabbit, or duck, and then vegetables or salad. The final course of the meal is

Italians tend to be close to extended family members and get together with them as often as possible. Here, three generations of a family enjoy an afternoon coffee together.

dolce, meaning "sweet," that is, dessert, which features delicacies such as tiramisu (layers of sponge cake soaked in coffee and brandy or liqueur) or gelato. "This may sound a lot like the Christmas dinner you prepare once every year," says Al Bacio, "but for Italians, this is a weekly event."[31]

For children, these family meals are a source of excitement and fun. They enjoy the hustle and bustle of meal preparation and the enticing aromas wafting from the kitchen. During the meal itself, children learn the pleasures of eating many varieties of delicious food and spending time with their relatives. "Italian children are reared at the table," writes Helen Ruchti in her book *La Bella Vita*. "They grow up sitting on the laps of parents, grandparents, aunts and uncles. They are held and kissed. They learn all the family stories and secrets of neighbors and friends. They learn to talk and listen simultaneously, to talk loud enough to be heard. They learn the joy of being with family and the value of a lazy Sunday afternoon."[32]

> "Children of every age are welcome in shops and restaurants, where shopkeepers and waiters happily chat with them."[33]
>
> —Julie Christensen, a writer and former teacher from Denver, Colorado

Kids Are Welcome

Italian children not only experience the joys of being with family at the dinner table but also are included in all types of family outings. Parents take kids along with them to art museums, historical museums, the theater, and a variety of cultural events. Children are encouraged, from a very young age, to appreciate the beautiful things for which their country is known. Italian children are welcome almost everywhere adults can go. "Children of every age are welcome in shops and restaurants, where shopkeepers and waiters happily chat with them," says Julie Christensen, a writer and former teacher from Denver, Colorado. "Visit a restaurant at 9:00 at night and you'll find extended families eating and talking."[33] Another common sight in restaurants is waiters picking up babies and cooing to them.

Changing Times

Although the importance of family is widely acknowledged in Italy, family life has changed a great deal over the years. One of the biggest changes from decades ago is family size, which has shrunk considerably. The familiar stereotype of the large, traditional family, with a houseful of young children, is no longer reality. In fact, says the Life in Italy website, "in the last thirty years the structure of the Italian family has dramatically changed from the traditional model we were used to see[ing] in old movies."[34] Today, Italian couples typically have only one child or two at the most.

Another change that has affected Italian families in recent years is the increasing number of mothers who work outside the home. A climbing divorce rate has resulted in the growth of single-parent families. And the economy is so weak that some experts predict it is on the verge of collapse. Such tough economic conditions have caused a severe shortage of jobs, which has forced many young adults to move away from their homes and families to find employment.

Yet despite these changes, and a necessity to adapt to new ways of living, Italians are resilient, optimistic, and determined. They have always been devoted to family, and they remain so. "Although traditional lifestyle is breaking down under the strains of modern life, family life in Italy still contains the seeds of past cultures," says Thomas. "Family ties are respected and Italians spend much of their time enjoying the company of their relatives."[35]

CHAPTER THREE

Education and Work

In August 2013, when exchange student Tommaso Giacomino arrived in the United States, he was captivated by how different it was from his native Italy. "Here everything is bigger," he says. "Houses, cars, hamburgers; and we don't have the idea of bottomless drinks or fries in restaurants." He also noticed how much bigger his American high school was than his hometown school. Giacomino soon learned that size was only one of many ways Italian and American schools differ. "Schools here versus there are almost from different planets,"[36] he says.

The Early Years

In Italy, compulsory (meaning mandatory) public education begins when children are six years old. That is when they enter elementary school, which Italians call primary school. Yet most children do not wait that long to start school. About 95 percent of children between the ages of three and six attend *scuola dell'infanzia*, or preschool. This is the equivalent of kindergarten, but it lasts for up to three years. "It is not mandatory," says Sarah, a girl from a small town just outside Milan. "But I've never met anyone who didn't start kindergarten when they were 3 years old."[37] Despite preschool not being mandatory, the government covers its cost. Every child is guaranteed a place.

Children in each preschool classroom are under the care and guidance of two teachers. Full uniforms are not required, but children must wear a smock known as a *grembiule* that covers their street clothes. For preschool boys, these smocks are usually blue-and-white checked. Girls' smocks are pink- or red-and-white checked. These can be purchased from most clothing

> "Schools here versus there are almost from different planets."[36]
>
> —Tommaso Giacomino, an exchange student from Rome

shops and supermarkets. If children want the smocks personalized with ribbons, embroidered names, or other adornment, parents can arrange to have that done.

While attending preschool, children spend their time playing and socializing with each other. Although they are having fun during their playtime, they are also learning. Music, dance, and physical activity are part of the curriculum, as are arts and crafts. A teacher describes one activity that kept eight children busy at a preschool in the northern town of Reggio Emilia. They were seated at a table working with large pieces of clay. In the center of the table was a plastic dinosaur, and the children were using the clay to build a habitat for the creature. In another area, two young boys were working with wood blocks, rocks, and disks of wood. At first the teacher did not know what they were building, but then, she says, "they brought out the giant predators—an alligator and a t-rex—and carefully constructed enclosures to keep them contained. At that point I thought they were only penning-in predators but later noticed that a giraffe was cordoned off in a corner. It was a zoo!"[38]

Along with learning through playing, preschool children also start learning how to recognize letters and numbers, often by singing songs and playing games. What they do in preschool can help build a foundation for their education. It can also help prepare them for primary school.

Primary School

When children are six years old, they start primary school, or *scuola primaria*. There is usually at least one primary school in every town, including small towns. Parents may choose any school they prefer rather than having to send their children to the school closest to home. The schedule varies by the school, but most students attend from about 8:00 a.m. to 1:30 p.m. Monday through Friday, and 8:00 a.m. to noon on Saturday. Children get a break in the midmorning to eat a snack that they have brought from home. "I usually bring a piece of plain white pizza," says a girl named Ilaria Rizzi. "It's topped with ricotta cheese instead of tomato sauce." After her snack, says Ilaria, "I get a few minutes to play."[39]

During the five years of primary school, children remain in the same classroom. Class sizes usually range from ten to twenty-five students. Like younger children in preschool, primary school students wear a *grembiule* over their street clothes. In primary school, however, boys and girls usually wear the same type of smock in a deep blue color.

Some of the first lessons in primary school are reading and writing as well as cursive writing. "Italy is one of the few Western countries where you are still taught to write 'in corsivo,' in cursive also known as longhand, script, joined-up writing,"[40] says Italian writer Katia Amore. A variety of other subjects are also taught in primary schools. These typically include Italian, English, and sometimes another foreign language. Other subjects include mathematics, science, history, geography, social studies, information technology, art, and music. In addition, most primary schools offer Catholic religious instruction once or twice a week. Students who practice other religions, such as Judaism or Islam, may opt for different types of classes instead.

Students wait outside their high school for the doors to open on the first day of classes in the city of Benevento. High schools in Italy are intended only to provide an education, so they do not offer extracurricular activities such as sports and clubs.

Secondary School

After five years of primary school, students undergo an evaluation. If they are determined to be ready, they can enter secondary school, or *scuola secondaria*. By the time they reach this level of schooling, young people no longer have to wear smocks over their street clothes. "Students in secondary school can wear whatever they want," says Amore, "even though it always turns into a non compulsory 'jeans and a T-shirt' voluntary uniform."[41]

Secondary school is often held from 8:00 a.m. to about 1:30 p.m., Monday through Saturday. This can differ from school to school, however, as Italian teen Sarah explains: "I used to leave the house at 7 in the morning and I wasn't back until 5 pm." Secondary schooling is split into two phases. The first, which lasts for three years, is known as lower secondary school. Also called

A Fun and Worthwhile School Project

Although secondary school in Italy is tough, students do work on projects they find enjoyable. In 2016, for instance, a group of middle schoolers from Mosso, a small town in the Alpine province of Biella, undertook an aggressive fund-raising activity. After reading a news story for a class assignment, they learned about an uninhabited island called Budelli that was for sale. Budelli is located off the coast of Sardinia in the Mediterranean Sea and is famous for its pink sandy beaches and unspoiled natural beauty. The kids from Mosso were concerned that the island would be sold to someone who would not preserve its natural beauty. So they decided to make it their goal to buy it themselves.

The students started a crowd-funding campaign to raise 3 million euros ($3.3 million) to buy the island. They are convinced that Budelli would make a perfect youth paradise that they would name Isola dei Ragazzi, meaning "the Children's Island." They have calculated that if every student in Italy donates just 50 euro cents, they can raise enough money to achieve their goal. "Our message is this: if all Italian students donate 50 cents, we could put together the 3 million euro needed to win the next auction," the middle schoolers told the newspaper *La Stampa*. "So that we avoid this heritage site becoming a stranger's private property."

Quoted in *Sputnik News*, "Italian Schoolkids Make Plans to Crowdfund Mediterranean Paradise Island," February 20, 2016. https://sputniknews.com.

scuola media, it is the equivalent of middle school. The second phase, upper secondary school, or *scuola secondaria di secondo grado*, is the equivalent of high school and lasts for five years. "Yes, you've heard right: 5 very long years!"[42] says Sarah.

Throughout the eight years of secondary school, students must purchase their own textbooks. This can be expensive, so many buy their books secondhand. They carry the books to and from school in book bags or backpacks, which are often stuffed and heavy. "I can assure you that our backpacks weigh a lot,"[43] says an Italian student named Lucrezia Ricciardello.

Classroom size in secondary schools averages twenty-one students. Students do not go from room to room for their classes. Rather, they stay in the same room and teachers move to different rooms to teach their respective subjects. "This will give you the chance to bond with every kid in your class," says Maria Teresa, a teenage girl. "You'll find amazing friends that will help you through out the year, because well, we are Italians, therefore really sociable."[44] In some schools, students are in the same classroom, with the same classmates, for the entire three years. Or they may be together for one year and then change to a new room.

Because students remain in the same classroom for the entire day, they have no need for lockers to store books and other belongings. So schools do not furnish lockers. Instead, students keep their coats, book bags, and other personal items with them in the classroom, often tucking their things under desks.

Middle School, Italian Style

Lower secondary school features a curriculum that expands on what was taught in primary school. This includes Italian (literature, grammar, and writing) as well as mathematics, physics, chemistry, natural sciences, history, geography, and social studies. Other subjects in the curriculum are physical education, a foreign language (usually English), technical drawing, music, religion, and art/design.

After three years of lower secondary school, students are ready to move up to the next level—but not until they pass a series of tough exams. These include both written and oral tests and cover all the subjects that were studied during the previous year. Students who pass these exams earn a diploma called the *licenza media*. They can then advance to upper secondary school.

No-Frills Education

Many Italian students feel like the high school years drag on forever because of how tough they are. "Honestly, the Italian school system belongs to another world," says student Lucia Bezzato. Bezzato says one of the toughest aspects of high school is having to attend six days a week. "We have only one day off," she says. "This is the reason why Italian teenagers are . . . exhausted and sleep deeply during the night. Sometimes you may be so 'possessed' by school that your night could become a giant nightmare where teachers are following you with a magic wand."[45]

High school is not particularly fun for students in Italy—but it is not intended to be. Students learn from an early age that they go to high school to get an education. "In Italy we go to school only to study,"[46] says a teen from southern Italy named Virginia. Students do not get to choose elective classes based on their personal interests or what they want to study. Rather, their classes are chosen for them on the basis of the type of school they attend. They take oral exams and/or written tests nearly every day. There are no school sports teams, no stadiums or athletic fields, and no gymnasiums. Schools do not have clubs, bands, theater groups, newspapers, or any other kinds of extracurricular activities.

The solemnity of high school is reflected in the attitude and behavior of teachers. They are strict and formal, and they expect students to take school seriously. They are not known for being friendly or approachable, they do not offer extra help or tutoring after school, and they make it clear that their only job is to teach. "You see," says a teen named Marta, "in Italy, a teacher is that person behind the desk that you probably are scared of more than everything else, that you need to respect and that plays such an important role in your life, being an educator and the source of most of [the] knowledge and life experience you will need later on in your college years and in your whole life too."[47]

Preparing for the Future

One unique characteristic of Italy's high schools is how career focused they are. In fact, Italy is one of the few countries where a choice about a student's future career is made before he or she enters high school. During the students' last year of middle school they choose the type of specialty high school they want to attend. This is often done along with guidance and advice from their teachers. "At the age of 13 you choose what you want to 'do for the rest of your life,'" says Gabriele More, a teen from Bergamo in the northern region, "because the high schools in Italy aren't the same as each other. If you like chemistry you can pick a chemistry school where you will study chemistry along with other subjects like Italian, math, and history, (you can't choose your subjects) for five years."[48]

More's comment about high schools not being the same as each other refers to how specialized high schools are. These schools fall into three broad categories: *liceo*, *istituto tecnico*, and *istituto professionale*. A *liceo*, which simply translates to "high school," is a college-track school. These focus on general or theoretical learning as opposed to technical or professional training. The *liceo* pathway branches off in different directions, such as *liceo artistico* (design, fine arts, and photography); *liceo classico* (classical languages, philosophy, and literature); and *liceo scientifico* (sciences such as biology, chemistry, and physics).

An *istituto tecnico* is designed to train students for a career after graduation. These types of schools focus on technical skills such as mechanics, logistics, and electronics. One branch of this specialty prepares students for careers in business administration, computer science, accounting, marketing, and tourism. Similarly, the *istituto professionale* offers vocational training that can help students go to work after graduation. Such jobs might include technical assistance, health care, and maintenance. "In Italy," says More, "you are formed as a worker in high school and after five years you are ready to get a job."[49]

When students have completed their high school requirements, there are additional steps they must take before graduating. "To graduate we have a huge exam that lasts for four days

> "At the age of 13 you choose what you want to 'do for the rest of your life.'"[48]
>
> —Gabriele More, an exchange student from Bergamo

Students prepare for the stringent exams they must pass to graduate from high school. Upon graduation, about 60 percent of young people choose to enroll in one of Italy's many colleges and universities.

about everything you have learned during your 5 years of high school," says Bezzato. "If you do not pass it, you have to repeat your last year!"[50] One segment of the exam is a series of written tests. This involves writing an essay on a topic related to literature, history, or science and a second essay on a student's chosen specialization. The third task is a written examination about several subjects the student has studied in the past year. Next, students take an oral exam in front of a group of teachers. The purpose of this exam is to determine whether the student has matured enough during high school to be able to discuss various issues intelligently and confidently.

Higher Education

Upon successful completion of all exams, students are awarded their high school diploma, or *diploma di maturità*. They can either go to work in their chosen profession or enroll at a university, which about 60 percent of Italian high school graduates choose to do. Italy has about ninety colleges and universities, more than half of which are publicly funded. Every major city and town has a public or private university.

While Emilia was in Italy, she attended the University of Pavia, located in the northern town of Pavia. Founded in 1361, the university is one of the world's oldest academic institutions. An estimated twenty-four thousand students attend it. According to Emilia, the work is hard and the study hours are long. And when exams roll around, it is a very stressful time for students. "The Italian exam season is a unique breed," she says.

> It's not the short week of finals in America and it's not the roughly two weeks for mid-winter exams in England. At *l'università di Pavia* we have nearly two months for January and February exams. You heard me correctly, TWO MONTHS. Your first exam could take place as early as 7 January and your last exam could be on 22 February. That's a long stretch of self-discipline to endure.[51]

Bleak Prospects

Young Italians who graduate from college are often dismayed and discouraged by the severe job shortage. In fact, the employment situation is so dismal that tens of millions of young people have left the country to find work elsewhere. Since the late 1990s, half a million Italians aged eighteen to thirty-nine have left for other European countries. To make matters worse, the youth most likely to move away are those who are the best educated and the most highly qualified.

Irene Tinagli, an economics professor and columnist, says that young Italians have lost hope that things will get better. She says they are leaving their native country not necessarily because they want to but because they see no other choice. "Italian exports are on the increase," says Tinagli. "Not of hand bags or shoes or Parmesan cheese, but people, above all the young and the educated."[52]

For many Italian youth, the scarcity of jobs is one reason why they continue

> "Italian exports are on the increase. Not of hand bags or shoes or Parmesan cheese, but people, above all the young and the educated."[52]
>
> —Irene Tinagli, an economics professor originally from Milan

living with their parents for years after finishing college. This is true of Gaia Paradiso, a young woman who returned home after working for six months in Belgium. "I think our generation is suffering a lot from this," she says. "Because if you don't have a job . . . you cannot really live your own life. If you have a job, then everything follows. I don't want to be rich, but I would like to have enough to continue my life and build something." Paradiso is highly educated. She has a bachelor's degree in economics and business management and a master's degree in international management. She speaks five languages: English, French, Spanish, Portuguese, and Italian, her native tongue. She has excellent career experience. But, she says, "sometimes it feels like it's never enough, like I cannot really find my place in this world."[53]

A Rapper Who Raps About Hope

It is an unfortunate reality that the job situation for young people in Italy is bleak—very bleak. More than 40 percent of Italian youth cannot find work, and in some regions, such as Campania in the south, the unemployment rate is even higher. So when Italian rapper/hip-hop artist Clementino released a song about hope called "O' Vient," which means "The Wind," his young fans welcomed the message he was sending them. "O' Vient" is about the hopelessness and desperation felt by many Italian youth who have tried and failed to find work. Clementino understands what they are going through because he grew up in the Campania region himself and saw the desperation firsthand. In his song he talks about being a voice for those who have nothing, and he encourages young people to stay hopeful and never give up on themselves. One of his fans is Giuseppe Forino, a young man who is unemployed and who says that Clementino's music speaks to him. "Coming from where he came from, a rundown little town, it's difficult to get noticed," says Forino, "but he did it. He's great."

Quoted in Zanna McKay, "This Rapper Speaks to Italy's Unemployed Youth," PRI, May 1, 2014. www.pri.org.

High youth unemployment rates have prompted many young people to leave Italy in search of better jobs elsewhere, while those who stay may be able to find only menial jobs. Here, a young man serves pizzas in Naples.

So Much Uncertainty

Young people who grow up in Italy are well educated through the public school system. By the time they graduate from high school, they have an excellent foundation for their future. But as true as that may be, the best education in the world cannot make up for a weak economy and soaring youth unemployment rates. Hopefully, things will improve in the coming years so Italian youth can once again live and work in their native country.

CHAPTER FOUR

Social Life

School is difficult and stressful for Italy's young people. They must endure hours of studying and homework, a six-day school week, seemingly endless (and grueling) tests, and constant pressure to do well. This, of course, takes up a huge chunk of their time. So when these young people have free time, they are eager to leave schoolwork behind and do things that they enjoy. Exactly what Italian teens like to do in their free time depends on their personal interests. In many cases, they enjoy doing the same types of things as teens from other countries: they get together with friends, watch television, read books, and hang out on social media.

In February 2017 a teacher from northern Italy, Simonetta Galli, posted an online survey of middle school students. The students answered questions about what they most enjoy doing in their free time. The most popular activity was listening to music, with pop and rap being the two favorite types. The teens also said they enjoy playing sports (especially soccer), using their smartphones, going out with their friends, watching television, and reading books. Other activities they mentioned were watching videos on YouTube, playing computer games, and going to movies. Of those who enjoyed reading, fantasy, horror, and adventure were their favorite genres.

Popular Piazzas

Italians are well known as social people. They are friendly, boisterous, animated, and often loud. They love to have a good time. This applies to Italians of all ages, including teens, who enjoy having fun and being with their friends. Italian teens often get together and do things in groups, and this is true whether they are dating or simply hanging out with good friends. They may decide to go eat at a *paninoteca*, which is a type of sandwich shop; go out for pizza at a pizzeria; or stop by a gelateria for a dish of delicious gelato. Or, perhaps they decide to attend a concert, go to a cinema to watch a movie, see a live stage play, or attend some sort of themed festival. If Italian youth are sixteen or older, it is legal for them to purchase beer or wine but not liquor. So they might visit a *birreria*, or pub, where they can talk, laugh, and dance to the music of a DJ.

Often, groups of teens have fun simply hanging out in the local piazza. Found in cities and towns throughout Italy, piazzas serve as the heart of a city and as the main gathering place. They attract people of all ages and all walks of life. In piazzas, children kick soccer balls around or play with their dogs. Adults can sit and relax with their newspapers over a cup of cappuccino. Teens can gather to have a good time with their friends. Getting together in the piazza is a common Friday night activity for Italian youth, says Luca Bottaini, a young man from Bologna. "Students go to the center of the city," he says. "During the summer there is a big screen [set up] and we watch films outdoors in the square."[54]

The historic Piazza di Spagna in Rome (pictured) is just one of many piazzas found throughout the city and the nation. These spaces serve as gathering places for people of all ages, where they can play, socialize, and relax.

Summer is also a time when open-air concerts are held in piazzas, as are carnivals and other forms of entertainment.

For teens who live in Florence, the Piazza Savonarola is a popular place to hang out. During the day and night, it is filled with people. When school lets out for the day, children go to the piazza to play sports and games. After the sun sets, local teens and university students meet up there. "We use Facebook messages or texts to coordinate," says a teen named Daniele, "but regardless, we are always meeting at the same spot in the piazza. And even if your particular friends are not there, you will always find someone to talk to."[55] As the evening wears on, the Piazza Savonarola is buzzing with activity—and lots of noise.

From Museums and Biking to Shopping

Along with hanging around piazzas or doing other fun things with their friends, teens participate in many other types of activities. Bicycling is popular with young people, both as a mode of transportation and for exercise and sport. Those who live in mountainous areas, which are plentiful, may enjoy hiking. Or they may prefer mountain biking. Stefano Calvagno, a teen from Sicily, has been involved in the sport since he was young. "Mountain biking really became my thing," he says, "because in Sicily we have a volcano (Mount Etna) that we bike. I even competed in nationals."[56]

> "Mountain biking really became my thing because in Sicily we have a volcano (Mount Etna) that we bike."[56]
>
> —Stefano Calvagno, a teen from the island of Sicily

Teens also like to spend time doing quieter activities, such as reading or visiting museums. They may spend afternoons sunbathing at one of Italy's gorgeous beaches. Or they may prefer to take long walks to explore and appreciate Italy's cultural riches. "Most of the cities are smaller and you can really just walk everywhere," says teen Maria Teresa. In the process, she says, "you will basically be walking through history, our cities are thousands of years old and full of art!"[57]

Maria also likes to get together with her friends when school gets out for the day. Like other teens in Italy, her school day ends in the early afternoon. "Most of the school[s] in most of the cities

Money for Culture

In November 2015, after the terrorist attacks in Paris, France, government officials in Italy became concerned about their country's youth. Specifically, they worried that terrorist groups such as the Islamic State (commonly known as ISIS) could lure young people away from their country and families and persuade them to take part in terrorist activities. To help deter this, former prime minister Matteo Renzi announced a cultural incentive program for the country's 575,000 teens. Upon reaching the age of eighteen, they would be eligible to receive 500 euros (about $550) that could be used for almost any form of cultural activity. This could include visiting Italy's resplendent archaeological sites, its numerous museums and art galleries, or its opera houses and theaters. The money could also be used for attending concerts, seeing live performances, or buying books.

Renzi's rationale for the cultural bonus was that terrorism must be fought not only by police officers, border guards, and intelligence agents but also by a strong affirmation of the cultural values for which Europe is known. "This is a bonus for kids coming of age," says Renzi. "Give them the symbolic awareness of what it means to be an adult in Italy—a main protagonist and heir of the greatest cultural heritage in the world."

Quoted in Nick Squires, "Italian Teenagers to Receive €500 'Cultural Bonus' from Government," *Telegraph* (London), August 23, 2016. www.telegraph.co.uk.

are in the city center," she says, "so every place where you can eat is at a walking distance. (Amazing, isn't it?)" By "city center," Maria is referring to retail areas with shopping and restaurants. "It's the same as a mall, but you're not inside a building, you're walking around the city," she explains. "So if you decided to hang out with your friends and go get an ice cream, you may find yourself trying some clothes on."[58]

Italian teen Jade Zhang also likes to go shopping in her free time. She and her family live near Milan, which is known as Italy's fashion capital and one of the leading fashion cities of the world. Zhang and her younger sisters enjoy shopping together. And whenever they go shopping, they never have to drive. "Students can go anywhere on public transportation,"[59] says Zhang.

Many teens have a wide variety of interests and are involved in many different activities. A teenage girl named Alice

A young biker takes a break to enjoy the view in northern Italy's Aurina Valley. Biking is popular among Italian teens, both for exercise and sport and as a means of transportation.

(pronounced Ah-LEE-che), who is from the town of Samarate, near Milan, has a very busy schedule. She takes dance classes five days a week after school. She also takes flute lessons and enjoys going to the theater, among other activities.

Angela Bogotto is another teen who really likes to keep busy—which is obvious by how packed her schedule is. "I really dislike having nothing to do," she says. Bogotto is from a small city in northeastern Italy called Schio. When she is finished with school for the day, she gets busy with one of her many activities. Some of her favorite pastimes include reading, writing, watching movies, and cooking. She is involved with scouts and often participates in fun activities with her scout group. She also enjoys skiing and dancing as well as playing the guitar and piano. But Bogotto's greatest passion is singing. She sings in a band and with a choir, and she also sings when she is by herself. "I sing everywhere," she says. "If I don't sing for a day I become crazy!"[60]

Fun with Technology

Like all teens, Italian youth like to stay in touch with their friends, and technology makes that easier than ever. Cell phones, especially smartphones, are common possessions of young Italians. They use their phones for everything from texting to hanging out on social media sites. In 2014 researchers conducted a survey to better understand how many teens have cell phones and how they use them. They interviewed young people aged nine to sixteen from Italy and seven other countries. The kids were asked whether they have a cell phone, and more than 68 percent reported they did. Most of those youth reported having smartphones, and slightly more than one-third said they have other kinds of cell phones.

Another finding was that the ways Italian kids use their phones is typical of young people almost everywhere. Those who could get on the Internet with their phones used them in a number of ways. For instance, they watched and/or recorded videos. Sometimes they played online games, either by themselves or with other young people. Another common way they used the Internet was studying for school. They also used video chat apps like Skype to have face-to-face conversations with friends and family.

> "I sing everywhere. If I don't sing for a day I become crazy!"[60]
>
> —Angela Bogotto, a teen from the northeastern town of Schio

Nearly all the Italian youth who accessed the Internet with their phones were active on Facebook or other types of social media. These respondents were asked about new friendships, and nearly one-fourth of them said they had met or started to communicate with new friends on social media. Like teens everywhere, those from Italy have their own favorite social media apps. According to one young man, Daniele Reda, the country's most popular social media app is Whatsapp, which is a messaging app similar to Facebook's Messenger or iPhone's iMessage. "If Italians can choose between iMessage and Whatsapp," says

Reda, "they'll use Whatsapp because everyone has it." He adds that Facebook is just as popular as Whatsapp among teens and adults: "So yeah, hands down Whatsapp and Facebook are the clear winners." Instagram is also very popular, says Reda, "but only between students (10–30 years old)." Another popular app is Snapchat, whereas Twitter is not very popular. "I mean, many people have it," Reda says, "but not so many people use it."[61]

Meet Lauren

Because social media is accessible throughout the world, teens in Italy can communicate with young people from many other countries. Some of them record videos of themselves and post them to YouTube. This is what an Italian girl named Lauren did in 2012. She made a YouTube video that she calls "Teenage Life

About 68 percent of young Italians have cell phones, most of them smartphones. Here, a group of friends poses for a selfie.

in Italy." She created it, she says, because people often wonder what living in Italy is like for teens. On her video, Lauren explains how she enjoys being with her friends and describes some of the things they do. Sometimes in the morning she meets her friend for breakfast at a local café on the nearby lakeshore. They order a typical Italian breakfast: cappuccino and a soft, buttery pastry known as brioche. Over breakfast, Lauren says with a grin, "we talk, we gossip a bit; you know, girls."[62]

When Lauren and her friends go out in the evening, they meet up at about 9:00 or 10:00 p.m. at a pub by the lakeshore. There they have a few drinks and are often joined by more of their friends. They spend a few hours talking and laughing together. Some evenings they go out dancing at teen nightclubs known as discotheques, or discos. If they do that, says Lauren, someone has to drive them. At the time of the video, neither she nor any of her friends were eighteen, which is the legal age to drive.

> "I can't live without soccer now."[63]
>
> —Stefano Sica, a teen from Naples

Italian Teens and Sports

Many Italian teens enjoy participating in some type of sport in their free time. By far, the most popular sport in Italy is soccer, which Italians call *calcio* ("football"). Stefano Sica is a teen from Naples who is passionate about playing soccer. He did not become involved in the sport until he was eleven years old, which is later than many youth in his country. But once he did, he was hooked. "I can't live without soccer now,"[63] says Sica.

Although scholastic sports do not exist, young people who are interested in playing sports have plenty of options. For soccer fans, there are youth soccer leagues, soccer clubs, and soccer camps for both boys and girls throughout the country. Anyone who wants to play soccer, regardless of ability, can play. And even though team members want to win, winning is not their focus. They mainly care about having fun. "In Italy, everyone plays . . . wherever there is time, space and a ball," says Ugo Rebecchini, a young man from Rome. Rebecchini started playing club soccer when he was ten years old and is now a star player in the United States. "The culture in Italy is all around soccer," he says. "There are no other sports that are as big."[64]

Soccer may be the most popular sport, but it is not the only one that interests young people. Tennis is also popular, and its popularity is growing, according to teen Stefano Trentini, who has played tennis since he was four or five years old. Trentini played at a sports club in his hometown of Ferrara. Club sports, he says, allow youth to play year-round and specialize in their favorite sport. They can play for different club teams, if they choose, and compete in tournaments against other club teams.

Unhealthy Activities

Sports and many other activities that Italian teens enjoy are fun and also good for their health and well-being. One common pastime among teens, however, is harmful to their health: smoking. A 2016 study found that nearly 40 percent of Italian teens smoke cigarettes, and kids were starting to smoke at younger ages—even before the age of thirteen.

When Jade Zhang first came to the United States as an exchange student, she noticed immediately how few people smoke. This is very different from what she was used to seeing at home. "In Italy, smoking is still popular," she says. Zhang estimates that 80 percent of young people in her country are smokers. From her American friends and host family, she learned that smoking was much more common in the United States in the past than it is today. As knowledge spread about how harmful smoking is to people's health, the practice declined sharply. "I hope in Italy it's going to be the same in a few years,"[65] Zhang says.

Along with smoking, many Italian teens are also involved in other harmful activities. A high percentage of them, for instance, are involved in gambling—and so are preteens. This was shown in a 2016 study in which secondary school students answered questions about their involvement in certain types of gambling, such as video poker and online betting. They also shared information about their experience (if any) with scratch-off lottery tickets.

The study findings revealed that 46 percent of boys and 35 percent of girls in sixth to eighth grade were involved with some sort of gambling. Scratch-off cards were the most common type, but online gambling was also prevalent among the young people. Even more astonishing was the close association between

A Kicking Star

When Stefano Calvagno was growing up in Catania on the island of Sicily, he fell in love with soccer. He played for his city team because Italian schools have no sports teams. He was aware of a sport in America called football, but he knew nothing about it. "I had never seen a game," he says. "It's like cricket. I know that someone plays cricket, but I don't know what it is." In the fall of 2014 Calvagno moved to America to attend high school in Massachusetts. Excited to learn that the school had sports teams, he won a spot on the junior varsity soccer team. One day during practice Calvagno caught the eye of the football coach, who told him that with his kicking skills, he should think about playing football.

When Calvagno returned to the school for his senior year, he decided to take the coach's advice and try out for football. Although he was intrigued by the sport, everything about it seemed foreign to him. "Just putting on the helmet was strange, the way it covers your head," he says. "That was the worst part." Calvagno made the varsity football team and soon proved himself to be so valuable that he was chosen as starting kicker. "I really am beyond excited," he says. "It's amazing, especially in my first year playing football. . . . I knew nothing about this sport, and I really didn't expect any of this to happen. But I am so thankful it did."

Quoted in David Willis, "Sicilian Sensation: Italian Exchange Student Stars as Rookie Kicker for Central Catholic," *Eagle Tribune*, December 3, 2015. www.eagletribune.com.

gambling and substance abuse. Gambling was reported by 60 percent of students who smoked, 73 percent who drank alcohol, and 63 percent who used marijuana.

It is alarming to Italian health officials that teens who use tobacco products or marijuana can now get those substances quite easily. In February 2014, for instance, a bar and café located close to the bus stop and train station in the city of Acqui Terme was caught selling cannabis products to teens. On their way to school, students could stop in and buy hashish and marijuana. The owner, Salvatore Nocera, was arrested after the high school principal noticed a strange smell in the school's bathrooms. He called the police, who found drug paraphernalia that led them to Nocera. One Italian news organization led a story about the situation with this eye-catching sentence: "A bar owner . . . has been arrested, after police found he was serving cannabis rather than coffee to students."[66]

Diverse Interests and Activities

Teens in Italy have a variety of personal interests and activities that they enjoy. These range from chatting with friends on social media or reading books to hanging out in a piazza on a Friday night, bicycling, or playing soccer in a league. And Italian youth sometimes make unwise decisions, although this is not unique to young people in Italy. All teens make mistakes and do things they may later regret. Hopefully they learn from their mistakes rather than repeating them.

CHAPTER FIVE

Religious Influence

Most children who are born and raised in Italy are Catholic. Although other religions are practiced in the country, Catholicism is the dominant religion. Families often display symbols of their Catholic faith throughout their homes. Pictures of saints are common, as are statues of the Virgin Mary and pictures of Jesus Christ on the cross. Catholics often wear crucifix necklaces and carry rosary beads, which are held during prayer.

The Roman Catholic Church is headquartered in Vatican City, which is a small city-state located in the heart of Rome. It is home to Saint Peter's Basilica and the Sistine Chapel, the latter of which is inside the Apostolic Palace, where the pope resides. Pope Francis I is the leader not only of Catholics in Italy but also of the estimated 1.2 billion Catholics worldwide. He is committed to serving Catholics of all ages, but he has a special place in his heart for young people.

Embracing Faith or Turning Away

Somewhere between 75 percent and 90 percent of Italians refer to themselves as Catholic. Yet only about one-third of them actively practice their religion. One 2005 survey found that fewer than one-quarter of Italian Catholics attend Sunday Mass. This percentage is even smaller among young people, according to Paolo Segatti, who teaches sociology at a university in Milan. Segatti surveyed a group of young Catholics and found that their attendance at Sunday Mass has declined sharply over what it was in the past.

Young Italians who have turned away from Catholicism have their own personal reasons for doing so. Many consider the Catholic Church to be stodgy, strict, and old-fashioned. This was the

> "I'm baptized and I do believe in God. I wouldn't leave the Church, even though I don't go very often at all, but it has lost a lot of appeal."[67]
>
> —Vincenzo Coscone, a student from Naples

problem for Vincenzo Coscone, a student from Naples. Yet he feels torn over it, as he explains: "I'm baptized and I do believe in God. I wouldn't leave the Church, even though I don't go very often at all, but it has lost a lot of appeal."[67]

Another young man, Francesco Lorenzi, has a very different viewpoint about his Catholic faith. Lorenzi plays guitar and sings with a popular rock band called The Sun. He went through a rough period of time when he was angry and depressed and abused alcohol and drugs. One night in 2007 Lorenzi's mother suggested that he attend a gathering of other young people at a local parish. He grudgingly went and is now delighted he did because it was a turning point in his life. "I saw a joy I never saw before and at a place I thought was for nerds," he says. "But it was the kind of joy I needed more than ever."[68]

Religious Traditions

Whether Italians regularly practice their Catholic faith or not, they observe many religious traditions throughout the year. One of the most important holidays is the Feast of the Immaculate Conception. On this day, which is celebrated all over the country on December 8, Italy recognizes the immaculate conception of the Virgin Mary within the womb of her mother, Saint Anne. As part of their celebrations, Italians often put up their Christmas trees and decorate their homes. "Everyone goes shopping and starts to prepare Christmas decorations," says Valentina Rossi, a teen from northern Italy, "and then we have the Novena (Roman Catholic tradition of prayers for [9] days) that begin nine days before Christmas. December 24 is used to spend time with family and friends and at midnight you have to go to church because this is when Santa visits the homes."[69]

Different kinds of religious rituals are also celebrated. For instance, a baptism (or christening) takes place soon after a baby is born. The ceremony is held in a Catholic church. Ahead of time, the baby's parents select a godmother and godfather, who accept the responsibility of ensuring that the child is raised to be a proper

Catholic. The parents send invitations to the baptism to friends and family. They also choose a location for the post-baptism celebration, which, in true Italian style, involves a delicious feast. This celebration often takes place at the parents' home but may also be held somewhere else, such as a restaurant.

In 2015 a baby named Marcello was baptized at a sixteenth-century stone church in the town of Castelluccio. The baby slept through most of the ceremony, in which he was blessed by the priest with holy water. Nearly forty friends and family members attended the ceremony and the celebratory *pranzo* (luncheon) afterward. According to Marcello's grandfather, Tom, the meal began with antipasti consisting of large plates of cold cuts, salamis, cheeses, bruschetta, and a dish called *roveja con pancetta* (wild

A priest baptizes a baby in Rome. The ritual of baptism is an important one among Italian Catholics. Friends and family are invited, and the ceremony is followed by a celebration that involves an elaborate feast.

peas with bacon). Two pasta dishes followed, and after those a mixed grill of beef, lamb, and pork was served. There were also side dishes of lentils, roasted potatoes, and fresh greens. Dessert, according to Tom, was a "to-die-for, cream-filled cake, colorfully decorated with a large AUGURI (best wishes) for *Bambino* Marcello."[70]

When Marcello and other children who are baptized Catholic get a little older, they will participate in another religious ceremony: their First Holy Communion. This usually takes place when children are seven or eight years old. Catholics believe that the First Communion is when the child and Jesus Christ are joined to become one. The boys wear suits and ties, and the girls wear fancy white dresses. The girls have their hair styled with flowers, beads, crystals, or other fancy adornment. In the past girls wore white veils, and some still do. Both boys and girls carry lilies and

Religious Studies Optional

Prior to the late 1980s Catholic religion classes were mandatory in all Italian schools, but that is no longer the case. Known as *Ora di religione* (religion hour), these classes are still taught in public schools but participation is optional. Although most students attend the religion classes, the numbers have been dwindling over the years. Growing numbers of parents and teachers question why state-sponsored schools should offer religious classes that focus on only one faith. Many teens are not in favor of religious classes either—and an incident in October 2013 made this abundantly clear.

At Christopher Columbus High School in Genoa, Italy, an entire class opted out of taking Catholicism. Never before in the country's history had such a thing happened, and supporters of religious studies were troubled by it. "These courses have value for everyone," says Friar Gabriele Mangiarotti. "If I want to understand St. Francis, or Dante, or Michelangelo, I have to understand the church. I honestly believe that students who opt out of the 'Ora di religione' are less prepared than the ones who take the course."

Quoted in Eric J. Lyman, "Italians Question the Merits of Catholicism Elective in Public Schools," *National Catholic Reporter*, October 30, 2013. www.ncronline.org.

candles. Families, and sometimes close friends, are invited to the ceremony. There is, of course, a celebratory meal afterward with multiple courses and plenty of delicious food.

In May 2016 second-graders at Marymount International School in Rome celebrated their First Holy Communion at the historic Church of Santa Susanna. Afterward, some of the children talked about the experience and how it made them feel. "I made my First Communion," says a little girl named Beatrice. "It was fabulous. We sang lots of songs. I read the prayer for the letters we wrote to God. I was nearly the last one to get communion. I liked the bread best. . . . The readings were very good, the singers sang very loud, and the people who brought up the gifts walked very slowly. I had a fantastic day!"[71]

> "I made my First Communion. It was fabulous. We sang lots of songs. I read the prayer for the letters we wrote to God."[71]
>
> —Beatrice, a little girl from Rome

Respecting Different Beliefs

Although Italy is a predominantly Catholic country, other religions are practiced there as well, including Judaism and Islam. As the leader of the Catholic Church, Pope Francis has stressed the importance of respecting people's different religious beliefs. Despite his commitment toward religious tolerance, however, religious discrimination is common and widespread. Muslims are especially discriminated against because of terrorists who attribute their atrocious crimes to Islam. This has continued to be a pressing fear because of terrorist attacks in France, Belgium, and other European countries. The fear has intensified as growing numbers of immigrants from the Middle East and North Africa have fled their homes, crossed the Mediterranean Sea, and arrived in Italy. "This has fuelled Islamophobia and anti-immigrant sentiment,"[72] says investigative journalist Lamiat Sabin.

In schools throughout Europe, including Italy, children and teens learn about the threat of terrorism. They also learn that many terrorists practice an extremist, militant version of Islam. Only a tiny fraction of Muslims are terrorists, but many people are convinced that Islam is a violent religion. This has increased fear and bigotry toward Muslims. In February 2015 Hamdy Hamisen, a Muslim

Egyptian student who lives in Milan with his parents, conducted a social experiment. He dressed in traditional Arabic clothing, wearing a long white robe and a white cap on his head. He carried a Koran (Islam's holy book) in one hand and prayer beads in the other. For five hours, with a video camera filming his actions, Hamisen walked around Milan—and was the target of verbal abuse. People yelled at him, accusing him of being a terrorist with the Taliban or ISIS. A woman pushing a baby in a carriage shouted at him. Groups of teens openly stared at him, astonished, and are seen laughing at him in the video. The video also shows a man standing near Hamisen at a train station, who remarks, "Look, he has got the Koran. Think he's got a gun under his tunic?"[73]

Religious discrimination is also rampant on college campuses throughout Italy. Muslim women, for instance, have been harassed for wearing hijabs, the traditional head scarves of women

A group of Muslim women celebrates a holiday in the Italian city of Turin. In Italy as well as other European countries, Muslims are discriminated against as the result of terrorists who attribute their atrocious crimes to Islam.

who practice Islam. In February 2015, female Muslim students attending college in northeastern Italy's Friuli-Venezia Giulia region were told they could no longer wear hijabs. This ruling followed racial violence against several Muslim students. According to the college's headmaster, "Outward signs of religion can be seen as provocation." In other words, he was claiming that if women appeared at school wearing hijabs, this could be viewed as inciting violence. Referring to the hijab, the headmaster declared: "They are free to use it outside school, but not in class."[74]

Homosexuality

Along with religious discrimination, Italy has a serious problem with bigotry against gay and lesbian youth and adults. Although the Catholic religion forbids homosexual behavior, this widespread bigotry is seldom related to religion. In fact, Pope Francis has condemned any type of discrimination against lesbian, gay, bisexual, and transgender (LGBT) individuals. He has even said that Christians should apologize to gay people for treating them so badly. Still, there are no laws to protect homosexuals from being discriminated against. This lack of legal protection, or even recognition, has created an unbearably painful situation for gay and lesbian youth. It has also contributed toward a disturbing number of suicides.

A lesbian couple who attends the same high school in Naples has endured physical and emotional abuse. The girls, Giulia and Laura, initially kept their love for each other a secret. When they decided to be open about their relationship, their nightmare began. Giulia's father beat her, saying that if she did not break up with Laura he would throw her out of the house. In school the girls were abused and bullied by principals and teachers as well as other students. "The vice principal said that I was turning the girls into lesbians, that it was a disease that I was spreading," says Laura. "During class, one of our teachers would say that we were disgusting, that we were abnormal. 'Does a hen mate with a rooster or another hen?' she would ask the class. Professors would stop my classmates in the hallways and tell them not to hang out with me."[75]

The girls reported the beating and the abuse at school. One teacher showed support, which helped them feel less isolated.

Their situation improved somewhat—but by no means is their relationship accepted by others. "My girlfriend and I can't hold hands in the street," says Laura. "One time we tried and people were threatening to beat us and rape us to 'bring us over to the other team.' This is the truth I live out every day, on the street, with my friends, and at home. . . . In the streets of Naples, Giulia and I can only ever be friends, and that's it."[76]

Teen Sexual Behavior

Heterosexual teens in Italy are not bound by the same expectations and societal norms as gay and lesbian teens. Still, however, Catholicism is strictly opposed to premarital sex. The church teaches that sex is acceptable only between a man and a woman who are married. "Catholicism considers sexuality an absolute taboo, and that sex before marriage or sex that does not result in conception is unacceptable,"[77] say the authors of an April 2016 study on teen sexual behavior. Yet even devout Catholics—including young people—disregard the rule, believing it to be outdated. In the same 2016 study, more than 60 percent of the youth, most of whom were Catholic, said they had already had sexual intercourse. On average, teens were fifteen years old when they had sex for the first time. When asked how much their religion influenced their sexual choices, only 16 percent said it played a substantial role.

> "My girlfriend and I can't hold hands in the street. One time we tried and people were threatening to beat us and rape us to 'bring us over to the other team.'"[76]
>
> —Laura, a lesbian teen from Naples

Another part of the survey involved talking with teens about sex education. Nearly all of them said that the school should play the most important role in sex education. But when asked about the sex education they received at school, 23 percent said that there was none. Due to traditional Catholic beliefs about premarital sex and birth control, there is no national requirement for sex education to be taught in schools, so few schools offer it. And of those students who had attended sex education classes, 36 percent of the teens rated them poor and only 9 percent said they were good. "The results obtained from our survey showed that there is an urgent need for sex education in Italy,"[78] the report's authors write. In an attempt to meet this need, in July 2016 Italy's Pontifical Council for the Family launched a new website called the Meeting Point. The site is intended to broaden young people's understanding of sex and the risks involved with being sexually active.

Some religious groups and individuals expressed outrage as soon as the site was launched. The conservative Catholic organization American Life League petitioned Pope Francis to take the site down, alleging that the material in the site was dangerous, inappropriate, and immoral. One of the angriest objectors was Phillip Mericle of the ultraconservative group Tradition in Action,

Building Houses, Not Walls

Religious leaders in Italy have searched for ways to help young people be more accepting of other faiths. In April 2016 members of a group called Pathfinder Ministries organized an event for teens of three different religions: Catholicism, Islam, and Mormonism. The purpose of the event was to build acceptance and understanding of different religions and to increase awareness of Europe's refugee crisis. Humanitarian groups have provided food, clothing, and shelter to refugees who have arrived by the hundreds on the shores of the Mediterranean. But many Italians are not happy about the influx of so many outsiders. This has led to widespread fear and discrimination.

The Pathfinder event, titled "A Culture of Hospitality," was held on a piazza in the northern city of Cesena. At the start of the afternoon each teen was given a cardboard box and was instructed to collect the various items that would be used during the scheduled activities. After collecting the items, the teens worked together to build houses out of the boxes. These houses served as symbols of inclusion, welcoming, and sharing. "At a time when new barriers are raised in Europe almost every day," says an article in the Seventh Day Adventist newsmagazine *Notizie Avventiste*, "the message that these children wanted to give is really strong: Instead of walls we have to build houses, that is, places where we are all part of a family."

Quoted in Andrew McChesney, "Pathfinders Build Cardboard House with Catholic and Muslim Teens in Italy," *Adventist Review Online*, April 19, 2016. www.adventistreview.org.

who stated: "The material offered in this Vatican sex education program is a saccharine cake mixed with poisonous filth."[79] Neither the pope nor the Pontifical Council for the Family agreed with the criticism, however. The site remains online and is considered a valuable resource for young people.

The Young People's Pope

As Catholicism has faded in Italy, and the number of practicing Catholics has diminished, many devout Catholics find this troubling. They fear that as more youth turn away from their religious faith, the religion will eventually die out. So when Francis became pope in 2013, Catholics were filled with renewed hope. They viewed him as the impetus that was sorely needed for Catholicism to be revived and to once again thrive.

From the very beginning Pope Francis made clear his desire to draw young people back to the Catholic faith. One way to do

Pope Francis has made a commitment to bringing young people who have strayed from Catholicism back into the church. Here, he poses for a selfie with a young girl in Rome.

this, he believes, is by moving the papacy (the office of pope) into a more modern age. Another is to reach out directly to youth. In August 2013 the pope held one of his first outreach events, summoning five hundred teens from a church group in Milan to the Vatican. When they arrived, Francis explained that he wanted to meet with them because they carry hope in their hearts; even though the teens live in the present, he explained, they are the "artisans of the future." He advised them: "Make the future with beauty, with goodness and truth. Have courage. Go forward. Make noise."[80]

Before they left the Vatican, the pope surprised the enthusiastic teens by posing with them for a selfie—the very first papal selfie. Others in the group took selfies as well—one photo after another was snapped with a cell phone. The photos were posted on Facebook and quickly went viral. Whether these outreach efforts on the part of Pope Francis will bring young people back to the church is not yet known. But he is committed to doing everything he can to help Italian youth once again embrace their Catholic faith.

> "Catholicism considers sexuality an absolute taboo, and that sex before marriage or sex that does not result in conception is unacceptable."[77]
>
> —An April 2016 study on teen sexual behavior

One young man who was surprised and delighted by a personal encounter with Pope Francis is Stefano Cabizza, a college student from Padua, Italy. He wrote a letter to the pope, but he did not expect a response; he simply wanted to communicate with someone he admired greatly. In the letter Cabizza wrote about his life and expressed his plans for the future, saying that he hoped to find a job when he completed his college studies. Once his letter was in the mail, Cabizza put it out of his mind—until the phone rang one day and the caller said, "Hello, it's Pope Francis." Cabizzo was amazed, especially when he learned that this was the second time the pope had tried to reach him. "I couldn't believe it," says Cabizzo. "He called me around five o'clock after finding that I was not at home the first time around." The two "laughed and joked" on the phone for about eight minutes, and Cabizzo was struck by the pope's humility and warmth. "He asked me to pray for him and then he gave me a blessing," says Cabizzo. "It was the most beautiful day of my life."[81]

A Changing Country

There was a time when nearly everyone in Italy was Catholic, and daily life revolved around the Catholic Church. Young people attended mass every Sunday with their parents, and families would not think of missing church. Although that is still true for many people, a growing number have pulled away from Catholicism. Italians still celebrate religious holidays and traditions, and these are an important part of their lives. But most no longer practice Catholicism on a regular basis. Devout Catholics hope that will change, perhaps with Pope Francis painting bold new strokes onto Italy's religious landscape.

SOURCE NOTES

Chapter One: A Country of Beauty and Fascination

1. Quoted in Peroni Italy, "An Interview with Photographer Giulio Pugliese." www.peroniitaly.com.
2. Ocean Malandra, "Facts on Mount Etna Volcano in Italy," *USA Today*. http://traveltips.usatoday.com.
3. Understanding Italy, "Regions of Italy." www.understandingitaly.com.
4. Quoted in Joy VanderLek, "Exchange Student from Italy Sums Up Cheshire Adventure," *Meriden (CT) Record Journal*, June 22, 2015. www.myrecordjournal.com.
5. Quoted in Sally Eyre, "Exchange Student Shares Taste of Italy with Family, Friends," *Arlington Heights (IL) Daily Herald*, April 27, 2016. www.dailyherald.com.
6. Marco Scognamiglio, "What Is It Like to Live in Italy?," Quora, December 8, 2016. www.quora.com.
7. Gaia Pianigiani, "You Say 'Anguria,' I Say 'Cocomero': Italy's Many Dialects," *What in the World* (blog), *New York Times*, October 8, 2016. www.nytimes.com.
8. Nicoletta Di Bartolomco, "Being Italian: An Insight into Italian Stereotypes," Just Landed. www.justlanded.com.
9. Giulia Rotunno, "With Love from Italy," *Outside In* (blog), February 27, 2013. https://smhsoutsidein.wordpress.com.
10. Passion for Italy, "People and Culture," 2016. http://passionforitaly.info.
11. Angela Bogotto, "Angela: Made in Italy," Port Lincoln High School, 2015. www.plhs.sa.edu.au.
12. Keith Hopkins, "Colosseum: Emblem of Rome," BBC News, March 22, 2011. www.bbc.co.uk.

13. Sylvia Poggioli, "Message from Italy's Failed Referendum: More European Uncertainty Ahead," NPR, December 5, 2016. www.npr.org.
14. Quoted in *Guardian*, "Italy Is a 'Dying Country' Says Minister as Birth Rate Plummets," February 12, 2015. www.theguardian.com.

Chapter Two: Home and Family

15. Di Bartolomeo, "Being Italian."
16. Bogotto, "Angela."
17. Jessica, "Help Improve My English in Borgosesia, Italy," Workaway, February 22, 2017. www.workaway.info/341119348717-en.html.
18. Quoted in Gaia Pianigiani, "Italy Baby Push Spurs Anger—Not 'Amore,'" *Atlanta Journal Constitution*, October 9, 2016. www.ajc.com.
19. Liz Fraser, "Parenting, Italian Style," Care.com, June 20, 2016. https://uk.care.com.
20. Quoted in Eyre, "Exchange Student Shares Taste of Italy with Family, Friends."
21. Quoted in Third Space, "Italian Family Life," October 14, 2015. https://3rdspaceproject.wordpress.com.
22. Michela Gatto, "About," *Green Candy* (blog), 2016. www.greencandylife.com.
23. Patrick Browne, "Why Half of Italy's Young Live with Mum and Dad," *Local*, September 16, 2015. www.thelocal.it.
24. Quoted in Browne, "Why Half of Italy's Young Live with Mum and Dad."
25. Luisa Angaroni, "Italian Exchange Student Makes a Queen City Comeback," UNC–Charlotte *Niner Times*, November 28, 2012. http://ninertimes.com.
26. Gaia Paradiso, "'I'd Love to Have My Own Place': Young Europeans on the Struggle to Fly the Nest," *Guardian*, March 25, 2014. www.theguardian.com.

27. Tommaso Giacomino, "Italian Exchange Student Describes First Days in Oregon," *CHI News Blog*, October 1, 2013. www.chinet.org.
28. Alison Jean Thomas, "Italian Family Life," Love to Know. http://family.lovetoknow.com.
29. Tuscookany, "The Pleasure of Eating Together the Italian Way," April 11, 2015. www.tuscookany.com.
30. Al Bacio, "Experience Sunday Lunch Italian Style," February 2, 2016. www.albaciobristol.co.uk.
31. Al Bacio, "Experience Sunday Lunch Italian Style."
32. Quoted in Charity C. Mathews, "5 Things Living in Italy Taught Me About Bringing Small Kids to Restaurant," Foodlets, February 1, 2016. http://foodlets.com.
33. Julie Christensen, "Italian Parents: 7 Secrets for Close-Knit Families," Education.com, November 20, 2012. www.education.com.
34. Anonymous, "Italian Families: Then and Now," Life in Italy, November 20, 2015. www.lifeinitaly.com.
35. Thomas, "Italian Family Life."

Chapter Three: Education and Work

36. Giacomino, "Italian Exchange Student Describes First Days in Oregon."
37. *Sarah in the Six* (blog), "Study Abroad in Italy? A Complete Guide to the Italian School System," November 7, 2016. www.sarahinthesix.com.
38. Kate Cicchelli, "BDS Visits the Diana Preschool in Reggio Emilia, Italy," Bennett Day School, February 2013. http://bennettday.org.
39. Ilaria Rizzi, "A Day in the Life: Italy," *Time for Kids*. www.timeforkids.com.
40. Katia Amore, "Back to School: 10 Things You Should Know About the Italian School System," *Italy Magazine*, September 12, 2014. www.italymagazine.com.

41. Amore, "Back to School."

42. *Sarah in the Six*, "Study Abroad in Italy?"

43. Lucrezia Ricciardello, "Italian High School vs. American High School," *Hillmen Messenger*, November 2, 2011. www.hillmenmessenger.com.

44. Maria Teresa, "When You Walk Through Italy, You Walk Through History," *Aspect Blog*, September 11, 2015. https://aspectblog.org.

45. Lucia Bezzato, "Differences Between Italian and American Schools," *Hilltop Echo*, November 14, 2011. www.thehilltopecho.org.

46. Virginia, "Exchange Student Comes to America," *Breeze*, September 15, 2015. http://smhsbreeze.com.

47. Marta, "Letter to Professor Anania," Liceo Classico Galluppi. www.liceogalluppi.net.

48. Gabriele More, interview with author, January 9, 2017.

49. More, interview.

50. Bezzato, "Differences Between Italian and American Schools."

51. Emilia, "How to Take an Italian Oral Exam (an Inexpert Guide)," *Emilia Lives Life* (blog), January 25, 2013. https://emilialiveslife.wordpress.com.

52. Quoted in Nick Squires, "Young Italians Abandon La Dolce Vita to Move to Britain," *Telegraph* (London), October 8, 2014. www.telegraph.co.uk.

53. Paradiso, "'I'd Love to Have My Own Place.'"

Chapter Four: Social Life

54. Quoted in *Las Vegas Review-Journal*, "Life in United States Offers Many Surprises for Italian Exchange Student," February 27, 2011. http://www.reviewjournal.com.

55. Quoted in Carmel D'Arienzo, "Lessons Learned from Life in an Italian Piazza," Plum Deluxe, June 29, 2013. www.plumdeluxe.com.

56. Quoted in David Willis, "Sicilian Sensation: Italian Exchange Student Stars as Rookie Kicker for Central Catholic," *Eagle Tribune*, December 3, 2015. www.eagletribune.com.
57. Maria Teresa, "When You Walk Through Italy, You Walk Through History."
58. Maria Teresa, "When You Walk Through Italy, You Walk Through History."
59. Quoted in Maria Norris, "Italian Exchange Student Shares What Surprises Her About Her Host Country," AuburnPub, March 23, 2013. http://auburnpub.com.
60. Bogotta, "Angela."
61. Daniele Reda, "What Are the Most Popular Social Apps in Italy?," Quora, November 5, 2016. www.quora.com.
62. Lauren, "Teenage Life in Italy," YouTube, July 27, 2012. www.youtube.com.
63. Quoted in Eric Shultz, "Varsity Voice: Tunkhannock's Sica Enjoys Onfield Success as Exchange Student," *Wilkes-Barre (PA) Citizens' Voice*, September 25, 2016. http://m.citizensvoice.com.
64. Quoted in Akilah Laster, "Let's Go with Ugo," *Inside the Lair*, October 4, 2016. www.calbears.com.
65. Quoted in Norris, "Italian Exchange Student Shares What Surprises Her About Her Host Country."
66. *Local*, "Bar Serves Cannabis Instead of Coffee," February 25, 2014. www.thelocal.it.

Chapter Five: Religious Influence

67. Quoted in Patrick Browne, "Losing Faith: Why Italians Are Spurning the Church," *Local*, January 8, 2016. www.thelocal.it.
68. Quoted in Michael Gresham, "Positive Feedback: Vatican Invites Rock Band to Explain Youth Culture," *Texas Catholic Youth*, February 8, 2013. www.texascatholicyouth.com.

69. Quoted in Joyce Hanz, "Holidays Away from Home: Exchange Students Soak Up American Christmas Traditions," Trib Live, December 20, 2015. http://triblive.com.
70. Palladian Traveler, "Marcello's Big Fat Italian Christening," October 3, 2015. https://thepalladiantraveler.com.
71. Quoted in Marymount International School, "Students Receive First Holy Communion," May 2016. www.marymountrome.org.
72. Lamiat Sabin, "Islam in Italy: Muslim with Traditional Clothes and Koran Insulted and Shouted at in Milan," *Independent* (London), February 19, 2015. www.independent.co.uk.
73. Quoted in Sabin, "Islam in Italy."
74. Quoted in *Iran Daily*, "Italian College Bans Hijab," February 19, 2015. www.iran-daily.com.
75. Quoted in Silvia Renda, "Suffering for Love: Giulia and Laura Tell Their Story of Homophobia in Naples, Italy," *Huffington Post*, February 2, 2016. www.huffingtonpost.com.
76. Quoted in Renda, "Suffering for Love."
77. Francesco Drago et al., "A Survey of Current Knowledge on Sexually Transmitted Diseases and Sexual Behaviour in Italian Adolescents," *International Journal of Environmental Research and Public Health*, April 2016. www.ncbi.nlm.nih.gov.
78. Drago et al., "A Survey of Current Knowledge on Sexually Transmitted Diseases and Sexual Behaviour in Italian Adolescents."
79. Phillip Mericle, "The Vatican's Depraved Sex-Ed Program for Youth," Tradition in Action, August 24, 2016. http://traditioninaction.org.
80. Quoted in Harriet Alexander, "Pope Francis and the First 'Papal Selfie,'" *Telegraph* (London), August 31, 2013. www.telegraph.co.uk.
81. Quoted in Nick Squires, "'Hello, It's Pope Francis': Italian Teenager Gets Surprise Phone Call," *Telegraph* (London), August 22, 2013. http://www.telegraph.co.uk.

FOR FURTHER RESEARCH

Books
Jean F. Blashfield, *Italy*. New York: Children's Press, 2013.

Kelly Davis, *Discover Countries: Italy*. London, UK: Wayland, 2014.

John Hooper, *The Italians*. New York: Penguin, 2015.

Thomas W. Paradis, *Living the Palio: A Story of Community and Public Life in Siena, Italy*. Bloomington, IN: iUniverse, 2014.

Tim Parks, *Italian Ways*. New York: W.W. Norton, 2014.

Internet Sources
Paddy Agnew, "Italy: Nice for Tourists, but No Country for the Young," *Irish Times*, January 9, 2016. www.irishtimes.com/life-and-style/italy-nice-for-tourists-but-no-country-for-the-young-1.2489777.

Katia Amore, "Back to School: 10 Things You Should Know About the Italian School System," *Italy Magazine*, September 12, 2014. www.italymagazine.com/featured-story/back-school-10-things-you-should-know-about-italian-school-system.

Lisa Miller, "7 Things Americans Can Learn from Italians," *Huffington Post*, November 6, 2015. www.huffingtonpost.com/2015/11/06/things-americans-can-learn-from-italians_n_4455377.html.

Organisation for Economic Co-operation and Development, "How's Life in Italy?," October 2015. www.oecd.org/statistics/Better%20Life%20Initiative%20country%20note%20Italy.pdf.

Websites
Italia per Gwen (http://italia4me.blogspot.com). The blog of Gwen Sawyer, an American college student who spent a semester in

2014 studying in Rome and who chronicles her experiences.

Italy Explained (www.italyexplained.com). An information-packed site that discusses Italy's culture, language, people, cuisine, and customs.

Italy Facts for Kids (www.kids-world-travel-guide.com/italy-facts.html). A concise collection of facts especially for young people, including information about Italy's geography, special attractions, language, cuisine, and people.

Italy Magazine (www.italymagazine.com). This site offers a wide variety of archived articles about Italy, ranging from how to speak the language and order food in a restaurant to information about the Italian lifestyle.

Life in Italy (www.lifeinitaly.com). This website offers a wealth of information about Italy, including geography, climate and weather, architecture, religion, schools, and culture.

Sienna in Italy (https://siennainitaly.com). The blog of Sienna Murphy, an American high school student who spent the 2015–2016 school year as an exchange student in Italy.

Understanding Italy (www.understandingitaly.com). Another information-packed site about Italy, Italian people, Italian life, and Italian culture.

INDEX

Note: Boldface page numbers indicate illustrations

Aeolian archipelago, 13
Alps, 9–10
Amatrice, 10
American Life League, 61
Amore, Katia, 33, 34
Angaroni, Luisa, 25
apartments, 27
Apennines, **6**, 9, 10
Apostolic Palace, 17, 53
architecture, 16–17
arts, 16–17

Bacio, Al, 28, 29
baptism, 54–56, **55**
Bartolini, Tiziana, 21
Il Bel Paese ("the Beautiful Country"), 8
Bezzato, Lucia, 36, 37–38
biking, 44, **46**
birthrate, 19, 26, 30
body language, 15
Bogotto, Angela, 16, 20, 46–47
Bottaini, Luca, 43
Browne, Patrick, 24
Budelli, 34

Cabizza, Stefano, 63
calcio, 49–50
Calvagno, Stefano, 44, 51
campanilismo, 12
Catholicism
  as dominant religion, 7, 53
  headquarters of, 17, 53
  number of worldwide members of, 53
  and religion classes in public schools, 33, 56
  traditions of, 54–57
  and views on sex, 60, 61–62
  young people and, 53–54
  See also Francis I (pope)
cell phones, 47, 63
Cesena, 61
children, behavior of, 21
Children's Island, 34
Christensen, Julie, 29
Christopher Columbus High School (Genoa), 56
Church of Santa Susanna, 57
cities
  map of, **6**
  See also specific cities
city centers, 45
Clementino, 40
colleges and universities
  difficulty of, 39

73

high school preparation for, 37
percent of high school graduates attending, 38
wearing hijabs at, 59
Colosseum, 16–17
Cortona, **4**, 12
Coscone, Vincenzo, 54
Crescenzo, Luciano de, 18
cuisine, 18
cultural incentive program, 45
"Culture of Hospitality, A" (Pathfinder event), 61
currency, 7, **7**

Del Magno, Anna, 13, 22
Di Bartolomeo, Nicoletta, 15, 20
diplomas di maturità, 38
discrimination, 57–60
divorce, 20–21, 30

earthquakes, 10
economy
  aging population and, 18–19
  birthrate and, 26
  employment opportunities for young adults and, 39–40, **41**
  living arrangements and, 24, 25–26
  mothers working outside of home and, 30
  personal debt and, 24
  regional differences and, 14
  unemployment and, 19
education
  absence of extracurricular activities in, 36, 51
  early childhood, 31–32
  primary school, 32–33
  religion classes and, 33, 56
  secondary school, **33**, 34–38, **38**
  sex, 60–61
Elba, 13
Etna, Mount, **6**, 10, **11**, 44
Euromonitor International, 18

Facebook, 47, 48
family
  changes in structure of, 30
  divorce and, 20–21
  extended, 23–24
  get-togethers, 27–29, **28**
  importance of, 20, 23
  inclusion of children in, 29
  size, 29–30
  traditional roles in, 21, **25**
  women working and, 30
Feast of the Immaculate Conception, 54
flag, **6**
Florence, **6,** 12, 44
food
  importance of, in social life, 27–29, **28**
  McDonald's, 18
  postbaptism feast, 55–56
  Sunday lunch, 28–29
Forino, Giuseppe, 40
Francis I (pope), **62**

attempts by, to draw young people back to Catholicism, 62–63
on discrimination against homosexuals, 59
on importance of religious tolerance, 57
as leader of Catholics worldwide, 53
need for sex education and, 61–62
Fraser, Liz, 21

Galli, Simonetta, 42
gambling, 50–51
Gatto, Michela, 24
gender roles, 21–22, **25**, 30
Genoa, **4**, 56
Giacomino, Tommaso, 31
government, 7, 17–18
Grand Canal, 12
grembiule, 31–32, 33

Hamisen, Hamdy, 57–58
Herculaneum, 11
high school, **33**, 34–35, 36–38, **38**
hijabs, **58**, 58–59
Holy Communion, 56–57
homes, 24–27
homosexuality, 59–60
Hopkins, Keith, 17

industries, major, 7
Islam, 57–59, **58**, 61
Islamic State (ISIS), 45
Isola dei Ragazzi, 34
istitutos professionale, 37

istitutos tecnico, 37
Italy, basic facts about, **6**, 7

La Bella Vita (Ruchti), 29
Lake District, 12
language, 7, 15
La Stampa (Italian newspaper), 34
Leaning Tower of Pisa, 16
liceos, 37
Life in Italy (website), 30
Lighthouse of the Mediterranean, 11
literacy, 7
Lorenzi, Francesco, 54
Lorenzin, Beatrice, 19, 26
Lo Stivale ("the Boot"), 8

Malandra, Ocean, 10
Mangiarotti, Gabriele, 56
map, **6**
Marymount International School (Rome), 57
Mayes, Frances, 12
McDonald's restaurants, 18
Meeting Point (Pontifical Council for the Family website), 61–62
Mericle, Phillip, 61–62
Mezzogiorno, 12–14, **14**
Michelangelo, 17
middle school, 34–35, 37
Milan, **4**, 45
Monte Bianco, **6**, 9–10
More, Gabriele, 37
Morelli, Giuseppe, 24
Mormonism, 61
mountain ranges, 9–10

music, 40, 42, 54
Muslims, 57–59, **58**
Mussio, Gino, 13

Naples, **4**, 12
nicknames, 8
Nocera, Salvatore, 51–52
Notizie Avventiste
  (Seventh Day Adventist
  newsmagazine), 61
Novena tradition, 54
nuclear family, 20–21

Ora di religione, 56
"O' Vient" ("The Wind," song
  by Clementino), 40

Paradiso, Gaia, 25, 26, 40
Pathfinder Ministries, 61
Pianigiani, Gaia, 15
piazzas, 18, **43**, 43–44
Pisa, 16
plate tectonics, 10
Poggioli, Sylvia, 17–18
Pompeii, **6**, 11
Pontifical Council for the
  Family, 61–62
population, 7
  aging of, 18–19
  birthrate and, 26, 30
  emigration of young adults
    and, 39–40
  physical appearance of,
    15–16
pranzo della domenica, 27–29
preschool, 31–32
primary school, 32–33
Pugliese, Giulio, 8

racism, 57–59
Rebecchini, Ugo, 49
Reda, Daniele, 47–48
refugee crisis, 61
Reggio Emilia, 32
regions
  archipelagos and, 13
  employment opportunities
    in, 40, **41**
  home design and, 26–27
  Lake District and, 12
  language variations in, 15
  loyalty to, 11–12
  Mezzogiorno and, 12–14,
    14
  physical appearance of
    people in, 15–16
  Tuscany and, 12
religion
  Islam and, 57–59, **58**, 61
  Mormonism and, 61
  Pathfinder Ministries and,
    61
  taught in school, 33, 56
  tolerance of different, 57
  See also Catholicism
Renzi, Matteo, 17, 45
Ricciardello, Lucrezia, 35
Rinaldo, Giorgia, 10
Rizzi, Ilaria, 32
Roman Catholic Church. *See*
  Catholicism
Rome, **6**, **7**, **9**
  Church of Santa Susanna
    in, 57
  Colosseum in, 16–17
  first McDonald's in, 18
  location of, **6,** 12

Piazza di Spagna in, 18, **43**
   Vatican City in, 17, 53
Rossi, Valentina, 54
Rotunno, Giula, 15
Ruchti, Helen, 29

Saint Peter's Basilica, 53
Scognamiglio, Marco, 14
scuolas dell'infanzia, 31–32
scuolas media, 34–35, 37
scuolas primaria, 32–33
scuolas secondaria, **33**, 34–38, **38**
scuolas secondaria di secondo grado, **33**, 35, 36–38, **38**
Segatti, Paolo, 53
sexual behavior, 60–62
Sica, Stefano, 49
Sicily, **6**, 10, **11**, 44
single-parent families, 30
Sistine Chapel, 17, 53
smartphones, 47–48
Smith, Rachel Vermiglio, 23
smoking, 50, 51–52
Snapchat, 48
soccer, 49–50
social media, 47–48
sports, 44, **46**, 49–50
Stromboli, Mount 10–11
substance abuse, 51–52
Sunday lunch, 27–29

technology, 47–49, **48**, 63
"Teenage Life in Italy" (YouTube video), 48–49
teenagers. *See* young adults

tennis, 50
terrorism, 45, 57–58
Thomas, Alison Jean, 27, 30
Tinagli, Irene, 39
Tradition in Action, 61–62
Trentini, Stefano, 50
Tuscan archipelago, 13
Tuscany, 12

Understanding Italy (website), 11–12
Under the Tuscan Sun (Mayes), 12
University of Pavia, 39

Vaccari, Martina, 12
Vatican City, 17, 53
Venice, **6**, 12
Vesuvius, Mount, **6**, 11
vocational training, 37
volcanoes, 10–11

Whatsapp, 48
women
   and mothers working outside of home, 30
   Muslim, **58**, 58–59
   traditional role of, 21, **25**
World Bank, 14

young adults
   Catholicism and, 53–54
   cultural incentive program for, 45
   employment opportunities for, 39–40, **41**
   extracurricular activities of, 46–47

gambling by, 50–51
gender roles of, 21–22
homosexual, 59–60
population of, 7
and relationship with family, 20, 21, 24–26
sexual behavior of, 60–62
smoking by, 50, 51–52
social life of
  biking and hiking and, 44, **46**
  hanging around piazzas and, **43**, 43–44
  most popular activities in, 42
  shopping and, 44–45
  technology use by, 47–49, **48**, 63
  See also education
YouTube, 48–49

Zhang, Jade, 45, 50

PICTURE CREDITS

Cover: iStockphoto/ddb

6: Maury Aaseng

7: iStockphoto.com

9: iStockphoto/belenix

11: © Avalon

14: Antonio Pisacreta/Ropi/Zuma Press/Newscom

22: iStockphoto/AscentXmedia

25: iStockphoto/Juanmonino

28: iStockphoto.com/guenterguni

33: iStockphoto/lucamato

38: Shutterstock.com/Marco Prati

41: Associated Press

ABOUT THE AUTHOR

Peggy J. Parks holds a bachelor of science degree from Aquinas College in Grand Rapids, Michigan, where she graduated magna cum laude. An author who has written dozens of educational books for young people on a wide variety of topics, Parks lives in Muskegon, Michigan, a town she says inspires her writing because of its location on the shores of beautiful Lake Michigan.